Women of Design:
Quilts in the Newspaper 1928-1961

Women of Design:
Quilts in the Newspaper 1928-1961

by Barbara Brackman
Edited by Judy Pearlstein
Book Design by Kelly Ludwig
    & Renée LaRoe
Photography by Jon Blumb
Production assistance by Jo Ann Groves

Published by Kansas City Star Books
1729 Grand Blvd.
Kansas City, Missouri 64108
Copyright ©2004 by
The Kansas City Star Co.

First edition, first printing
ISBN: 0-9746012-9-2

Printed in the United States of America
by Walsworth Publishing Co.

To order copies, call StarInfo,
(816-234-4636)

www.PickleDish.com

PickleDish.com
The Quilter's Home Page

KANSAS CITY STAR QUILTS

Contents

Introduction 2

Acknowledgements 7

Getting Ready 8

Ruby McKim block 18

Eveline Foland block 28

Edna Marie Dunn block 38

Aunt Martha block 44

Work Basket block 58

Wheeler/Brooks block 70

Herbert Ver Mehren block 82

Carlie Sexton block 90

Rose Kretsinger block 104

Carrie Hall Block 112

Louise Fowler Roote block 118

Oklahoma Farmer
   Stockman block 124

Scioto Danner block 130

Designer Basket borders 138

Gallery 170

Bibliography 173

What's Black and White and Red All Over?
Barbara reveals the answer to the old
joke with a copy of *The Kansas City Star*
before Joyce Colton's *Black and White and
Re(a)d All Over.*

About the Author

Barbara Brackman lives in Lawrence, Kansas, in a
Victorian cottage full of the collections shown in this
book. Most of the photographs were shot in the house
where she's lived for thirty years. She's written
numerous books about quilts, including the recently
published *America's Printed Fabric: 1770-1890*. This is
her second book for Star Books. *Prairie Flower: A Year
on the Plains* appeared in 2001. She designs
reproduction fabrics for Moda®, a division of United
Notions. She's copied some of her favorite fabrics from
the 1930s and '40s in a collection of prints called
Patterns of History, a partnership with *The Kansas City
Star*. With Karla Menaugh she runs a quilt pattern
company called Sunflower Pattern Co-operative,
keeping alive the tradition of cottage industries.

Introduction

When I was a college student in the 1960s, I frequented
thrift stores looking for flapper dresses, cast iron toys,
hula lamps, tramp art picture frames, old quilts and
Fiesta Ware dishes. One day, among that abundance of
discarded treasures available at bargain prices, I found a
packet of newspaper clippings. Fifty quilt patterns from
The Kansas City Star - 50 potential projects for a dollar!

I've been collecting patterns ever since, although I haven't anything close to a complete set, estimated to total over 1,000 patterns. My *Star* clippings, filed in four notebooks, are one part of my rather substantial collection of old quilt patterns, a collection that continues to grow.

That first package of clippings set my life on an interesting course. At first, pattern collecting was a hobby. I entertained myself for uncounted hours sorting through the designs, shopping for new additions in antique shops and garage sales, and corresponding with fellow pattern collectors, many of whom have become good friends. In looking back, I realize pattern collecting was a therapeutic contrast to my job as a special education teacher. After a day of trying to organize a group of eight-year-old anarchists, I was pleased to be able to spend my evenings putting all my nine-patches in good order.

To my surprise, quilts are no longer a hobby. I now have a career as a professional quilt historian. In recent years, I've been thrilled to design my own patterns for *The Kansas City Star*.

In the year 2004, the monthly series has been devoted to the original sources, Midwestern pattern designers of the mid-twentieth century. Every month *Star magazine* printed a new basket pattern, an original design inspired by both a pieced basket and an appliqué floral from the designer of the month. I tried, in drawing these patterns, to keep the new pattern in the style of the old, including some of the features that made her designs distinctive.

Where the Wild Flowers Grow by Jean Pearson Stanclift, Lawrence, Kansas.

This book includes the monthly patterns from the 2004 *Star* with expanded biographies, a multitude of color suggestions and various sets and borders. I've also designed additional projects inspired by the designers' work and invited a few friends to show their ideas for other crafts.

This book offers much about the history of quilt patterns, not only giving you an opportunity to read about the designers and their careers, but also a chance to see a bit of their world in the photographs. In many of the photos, we've arranged sewing tools, fabric, fashion items, dishes and needlework of the era to give you a glimpse of the context of the times.

The Commercial Quilt Network

Kathy Delaney's *Red Hot Women of Design* quilt backs mid-twentieth-century collectibles including feedsacks, quilt blocks and a pattern scrapbook compiled by Josephine Salber of Waldo, Kansas.

The history of commercial needlework patterns is a story of women's work. The Midwestern companies described here were run primarily by women who designed patterns for the newspapers, who sold patterns in department store dry goods sections, who pasted up simple mail order catalogs and folded mimeographed designs into brown paper envelopes. Needlework pattern companies were often cottage industries - small businesses run from women's homes with the help of their sisters or their husbands, their mothers or their children and an occasional paid employee.

Related to the pattern sources were the needlework columns in the newspapers and magazines of the time, an empire managed by female editors, such as Louise Roote and Edna Marie Dunn, who made their careers in the women's section, discussing fashion or cooking. Their empires, of course, may also be viewed as a ghetto. Women were generally confined to the middle pages of the magazine or the "women's section" of the newspaper. Louise Roote was one ladies' page editor fortunate enough to stay in the business until World War II, when she graduated from the women's page to become general editor at

Capper's Weekly. Like many other wartime women, she took over a traditional man's job.

Several of the women you'll meet in these pages found needlework patterns to be remarkably profitable. Husband and wife teams, the McKims, the Tillotsons and the Ver Mehrens, found a way not merely to weather the Depression but to prosper. A few women, such as Scioto Danner and Carlie Sexton who lived without husbands to provide support, found managing a needlework company a prosperous alternative to traditional salaried occupations. Entrepreneurs like Danner and Ruby McKim were successful enough that *The Star* interviewed them to find their business secrets. Rose Kretsinger was one of the few designers who turned to patterns more as a hobby. Well supported by her banker husband, she sold an occasional hand drawn design for a few dollars.

The history of quilt pattern publication in America is generally traced to an 1835 article in *Godey's Lady's Book* picturing a hexagon design. Magazines sporadically printed quilt designs between 1835 and 1880 but it isn't until late in the nineteenth century that periodicals regularly referred to quilts, mentioning the current fads such as crazy patch and embroidered redwork. In the 1890's, references continued to increase. Quilt designs became a consistent feature of

the readers' exchange columns in women's and farm magazines. "Does anyone have a pattern for a Drunkard's Path?" one reader might ask, to be followed up the next month by a sketch of the block in question. These exchanges functioned much like the quilt computer lists of the 21st century that share patterns and techniques throughout the country.

In the early 20th century, periodicals began selling full-sized diagrams for the patterns that readers mailed in to the editor. The woman's page might picture a block and ask readers to send a nickel or dime for the pattern. This combination of pictured block and mail-order pattern became the standard periodical format for decades. Among Ruby Short McKim's many innovations was the idea of publishing the actual pattern to scale in the teens.

Magazine mail-order departments competed with companies devoted solely to selling designs through the mail. During the last decades of the nineteenth century, while Montgomery Wards and Sears, Roebuck and Company were taking advantage of rural free delivery to sell fabric, batting and quilt frames through the mail, pattern companies like the Ladies Art Company, run by H. M. Brockstedt of St. Louis, sold patterns. Brockstedt is credited with the first catalog devoted to quilt patterns, published in 1889.

Many of the designers celebrated in this book followed Brockstedt's lead with pamphlets picturing their inventory of designs, traditional and modern. The catalogs were often free, but quilters were also willing to pay a quarter for the advertising booklets, just for the chance to see photographs of blocks and antique quilts. Most seamstresses at the time had, like Carrie Hall, the pattern making skills to draft their own templates if they had a sketch or photo of the finished block.

In the late 1920s, newspapers around the nation responded to reader requests for a regular pattern feature. *The Star's* was among the earliest with the first appearing on September 22, 1928. Ruby McKim's design initiated a column that lasted until May 24, 1961 with the last of Edna Marie Dunn's many drawings. The pattern usually appeared in the Saturday paper and was repeated on Wednesdays in the weekly farm periodical published by *The Star. The Weekly Star Farmer,* also called the *Weekly Kansas City Star,* reached subscribers in Missouri, Kansas, Oklahoma, Colorado, Nebraska, Iowa and Arkansas.

In addition to their unique full-sized pattern feature, the paper also offered two different reader mail services, syndicated pattern features for mail order designs, a new quilt pattern format. Syndicated quilt columns began in the late 1920s and within a few years dominated the periodical pattern network. *The Star* was one of a very few papers that continued to run a unique quilt column featuring regional designs after the advent of the syndicated quilt column. Most, like *Capper's Weekly* and the *Oklahoma Farmer Stockman,* subscribed to the reader mail services operated by Needlecraft Supply, which sold designs under the name of Laura Wheeler, or Kansas City's Colonial Patterns, which used the name Aunt Martha.

The quilt revival that flourished from the late 1920s through the 1940s began to lose steam after World War II. Quilts were again perceived as part of the world of poverty, hand me-downs and country crafts, concepts quite unpopular in the 1950s. By 1960, most of the needlework companies were closed and the quilt columns, including *The Star's,* were replaced with television listings and Dear Abby features.

We are now, happily, again living in an era when quiltmaking is a fashionable hobby. The current quilt revival has created a revived demand for needlework patterns. A partial list of the women who run today's cottage industries in the Kansas City area includes Barb Adams and Alma Allen's Blackbird Designs; Amy Bradley; Gerry Kimmel Carr's Red Wagon; Lynne

Lynne Hagemeier's Kansas Troubles; Indigo Junction; Vickie Lawrence's Prairie's Edge Patchworks; Renee Nanneman's Need'l Love; Cherie Ralston and Jan Patek in Jan Patek Quilts; Karla Menaugh's and my Sunflower Pattern Co-operative; Terry Thompson's Peace Creek Patterns and Ruth Powers Innovations. Once again, the same creative energy that made the area a hotbed of design in the1930s is in the air.

Acknowledgements

Thanks to photographers Jon Blumb and Mark Hutchinson, book designers Kelly Ludwig and Renee LaRoe, editor Judy Pearlstein, and pattern artist Eric Craven, who shaped this book into its final form. And, again, thanks to Jean Pearson Stanclift who stitches the blocks that grace *The Star's* monthly patterns each year. While making the 2004 model and several of the smaller projects for me, she also found time to make her own version seen on the cover.

I gave several women the patterns early in 2004 and they miraculously came up with finished quilts and tops by the July deadline. Thanks to Shirley Brown, Susannah Christenson, Joyce Colton, Kathy Delaney (who made two!), Amanda Gilbert, Linda Harker, Carol Kirchhoff, Linda Kittle, Deb Lybarger, Denise Mariano, Pam Mayfield, Pat Moore, Deb Rowden, Debi Schrader, Nancy Wakefield, and Shirley and Shirlene Wedd.

And also thanks to the quilting part of the design team, Kelly Ashton, Linda Harker, Lori Kukuk, Lee and Becky Robertson and Jeanne Zyck, artists working from their homes who are a vital aspect of the area's continuing quilt heritage.

Getting Ready

The Designer Basket Quilt

Thirteen pieced and appliquéd blocks celebrate mid-twentieth century quilt designers who made mid-America the heart of quilt country. The patterns in the *Designer Basket* sampler reflect the style of Depression-era artists who helped shape the look of the twentieth-century quilt.

Choose a color palette that reflects your taste and decorating style. Color makes the quilt. Reproduction prints in clear, pale shades call to mind the mid-century classic quilt. But brights and batiks can make traditional design look brand new. Soft pastels in slightly subdued shades are up-to-date, while toned-down color backed by tan neutrals creates a quilt at home in "country" decoration. For color inspiration, you'll want to look at the many samples made by Kansas City area quilters in the pages that follow.

The yardage below for the various models generally includes estimates for the 13 blocks. You'll want to think about setting, sashing and borders so browse through chapter 14, choose a setting you like. Add the fabric estimate there to your shopping list.

A word about the patterns and measurements:

If you've ever made a friendship quilt you know that 20 different quiltmakers can come up with 20 different variations of a 9-inch measurement. We noticed when measuring the sample quilts, especially those with the blocks on point, that there was quite a variation in the border measurements. To insure that you have enough fabric, you are smart to cut your borders a bit long (as we tell you in the pattern instructions) and trim later if you need to.

A word about techniques.

This is a book about pattern and design, not about techniques. For a how-to course in quiltmaking, see Kathy Delaney's *Star* book *The Basics, An Easy Guide to Beginning Quiltmaking*. (To order, call 816-234-4636 and say "starinfo."). For more about the techniques of machine appliqué used by Jean Stanclift and several other appliqué artists, see *Quiltmaker's Guide to Fine Machine Appliqué* by Karla Menaugh, Cherie Ralston and Barbara Brackman (Sunflower Pattern Co-operative, 2002, (502) 222-2119.

Color: Thirties Reproductions

People commonly refer to the pastel quilts from the mid-twentieth century as "Depression Quilts," but the fashion for light clear colors in scrappy patchwork combined with a neutral of plain white cotton appeared before the 1929 stock market crash and the economic crisis of the 1930s. During the mid-twenties America was undergoing a different crisis of social changes. Women who bobbed their hair and shortened their skirts were ready to take up quiltmaking so long as the look was modern. Louise Fowler Roote, writing for *Capper's Weekly*, described the new color scheme, when she advised readers to piece an old pattern, "not in the brilliant red and green oil calico of colonial times, but in the soft pastel colorings of maize and pale green on an ivory background."

New dyes and new technology enabled fabric mills to give quilters inexpensive cottons printed in the whole spectrum of colors, a real change from the unreliable, dark cottons available through World War I. During the late 1920s, splashy prints covered

Designer Baskets by debi schrader, Kansas City, Kansas. 93" x 93". Machine quilted by Lee and Becky Robertson.

Debi appliquéd the flowers using a machine-made buttonhole stitch and black thread to give her reproduction quilt a true period look. During the 1930s, many quilters finished their appliqué with black embroidery. Her scrappy sashing is 3" strips; her inner border 3" and the outer white border finishes to 5 1/4".

with layers of stylized flowers were fresh and new. Art deco zigzags, plaids and stripes coexisted on the same fabric with tulips, daisies and pansies. The prints combined any number of shades but the recurring color theme was white. The majority of the dress prints from the time and the majority of the quilts made with those fabrics include white. The quilts therefore have a light appearance, despite the dark and bright details of the colors in the prints.

Although design principles weren't often written down, we can infer a few general rules by looking at the quilts of the time. Among them:

1) Any color goes with any other color.
2) The more colors the better.
3) The neutral is white, which usually dominates the quilt's color scheme.
4) The more prints the better.
5) Contrast, rather than focusing on light and dark, balances prints versus plains.
6) Colors were clear with little interest in a toned down or grayed palette.

Today, we have many lines of mid-century reproduction prints to give our quilts the nostalgic look of grandma's handwork.

Baskets

For the baskets, pick pairs of reproduction prints, either two shades of the same color, or think as they did back in 1933, and contrast print and plain. Dramatic light/dark contrast didn't interest Depression-era quiltmakers. They loved the subtle contrast of prints with plains.

To capture that look, stitch your baskets of two fabrics in similar shades, one a print, one a plain. If you want your quilt to look authentic don't stick solely with pastels. Add red, black, navy blue and a little brown to the mix.

Yardage:

You'll need variety for the 13 baskets. You can probably get two baskets out of each fat quarter, so buy the following:

8 or 9 fat quarters of plain (or medium shade)
8 or 9 fat quarters of print (or light shade)
1 striped fat quarter for "Carlie's Wild Rose" (see page 90)

Florals

Again, think prints and plains - or two shades of plain, a medium and a light. This is the place to make the most of the many plain-colored cottons we have right now in the clear shades so popular mid-century. If you want to include the whole spectrum they used in the 1930s buy 1/2 yard light and medium or print and plain of the following:

- yellow
- pink
- orange (peach)
- purple (lilac)
- blue
- green
- 3 extra fat quarters of green for the stems and leaves.

Backgrounds

The background in a 1930s reproduction should be plain white, possibly a shade of off-white as if the cotton has yellowed with age. Don't think "unbleached muslin." Quilters did use unbleached muslin and recycled sugar sacking if they had to, but the coarse cotton with its slubs and specks was not used for showy quilts like this basket sampler. If you love the look of unbleached muslin, realize that it's going to wrinkle and shrink more than a better quality cotton percale.

To update your look, think white on white print, a style that wasn't available back in the 1930s, but a unique contemporary look that adds a little texture to the background. You can also mix a variety of white and off white plains to obtain the appearance of an old quilt where the whites have yellowed in different fashion.

Yardage

3 yards of white for the block backgrounds. If you want a border of white, look in chapter 14 for border yardage.

Updating the Reproduction Look

Consider using a different background shade with the reproduction prints and plains. Black is always dramatic. You could reverse the rules and make your flowers in shades of white on backgrounds of clear pastels. If you cut out the fabric behind the appliqué you won't have a shadow behind the white.

Red Hot Women of Design by Kathy Delaney, Overland Park, Kansas. 64" x 64". Machine quilted by Kelly Ashton.

Kathy's captured the mid-century decorating palette of red and black by machine-appliquéing 1930's reproduction prints to a red background with a black buttonhole stitch. There's no border because the black edge triangles frame the designer baskets so well. She asked Kelly to quilt the setting squares by outlining the various monthly appliqués.

Designer Baskets, hand-appliquéd by Deb Lybarger, Lawrence, Kansas. 108" x 108".

Deb combined batik florals and baskets of Japanese imports, designing her own border on a 16" background with a 2" outer border of black. The quilt top resonates with Japanese inspiration, taking the 1930s basket blocks far from their Midwestern home.

Color: Today's Pastels & Monochromatic Prints

Baskets

For the 13 pieced baskets, pick 5 pairs of prints, a light and a dark. Most of the baskets are pieced of a single color in two shades. You'll have extra for appliqué.

Yardage

1/2 yard of two shades of the following colors,

- pink (rosy or peachy)
- purple (either lilac or raspberry)
- green (either teal or yellow-green)
- blue (go for sky blue or turquoise)
- yellow (yellow or peachy orange)
- 1 striped fat quarter for "Carlie's Wild Rose" (see page 90)

Florals

For the bouquets, add to your palette by choosing fat quarters of darker shades of the 5 colors for highlights, reds and oranges for flowers and greens for the foliage.

- 1/4 yard red
- 1/4 yard orange
- 2 quarter yard cuts of different greens so you have 4 greens in all
- 1/4 yard dark pink
- 1/4 yard dark purple
- 1/4 yard dark blue
- 1/4 yard gold

Kansas City Star Flower Basket Quilt by Shirlene K. Wedd and Shirley C. Wedd, Lawrence, Kansas. 90" x 90" The Wedd's hand-appliquéd quilt top makes the most of today's prints by combining naturalistic floral colors with baskets in browns on a single print background. The soft green stripe used for the setting and border background is a daring choice that works well. The border is their own design, made from their favorite flowers in the sampler blocks. The sashing is 2"; the border 9", the same size as the *Designer Basket* sampler patterned on page 150.

Backgrounds

In the early 21st century, the trend is a scrappy background look with different prints that are closely related in color but varied in scale and density. Shop for similar prints and don't forget geometrics such as stripes and plaids. Of course, you can use a plain colored fabric, especially if you plan some fancy quilting, but the prints give an extra texture to the blocks. For this contemporary look, choose background shades of a yellowed white or tan rather than clear white or blue or gray white.

You can, as the monthly newspaper pattern suggested, buy a fat quarter of background print for each of the 13 baskets. You'll just be able to get one background out of a fat quarter, if you cut carefully.

For a mixed background buy: 4 different off-white or tan prints, 1 yard of each.
If you prefer one piece of background fabric, buy: 3 yards of an off-white print or tan print

Designer Basket by Pamela Mayfield, Lawrence, Kansas. 90 x 90. Machine quilted by Lori Kukuk. Pam's quilt in pinks and browns is a perfect complement to today's country decorating fashion. The more muted the color, the more "country" the look. She mixed her backgrounds, even mixing them within the same block. The change of direction in her striped borders is another of her creative design ideas.

Color: The Hand-Dyed Look

Quilters who have no interest in dyeing their own fabrics have ample commercially-printed fabrics available. The swirly, painterly prints in rich jewel-tone colors are usually called "batiks." Not quite a solid color, batiks allow the designer to paint with the fabric, so they're a favorite for floral appliqués.

Baskets

To make 13 pieced baskets, similar to Carol Kirchhoff's, match pairs of brown batiks in light and dark. Most of the baskets are pieced of two shades. You'll have extra for appliqué.

Yardage

1/2 yard pieces of 6 shades of light brown batiks, 6 shades of dark brown batiks
1 striped fat quarter for "Carlie's Wild Rose" (see page 94)

Midnight Flower Baskets by Carol Kirchhoff, Shawnee, Kansas. 82" x 82". Machine quilted by Jeanne Zyck.

Carol, who owns Prairie Point Quilts in Shawnee, cut kits for her customers in these painterly prints that today's quilters call "batiks." Carol added drama with a black background and a simple green vine machine-appliquéd to the 3" sashing. Her machine appliqué features a buttonhole stitch in colors to match or contrast with the appliqué. Jeanne quilted an arabesque of feathers with green thread to create an overlay of subtle color.

On the wall is another quilt using commercial fabrics with a hand-dyed look. Shirley Brown's wall hanging of three baskets was machine-quilted by Linda Harker. Three baskets in a row with four edge triangles set between them finish to a wall hanging 21 1/4" by 63 1/2".

15

Blessings in the Baskets, hand appliquéd and hand quilted by Susannah Christenson, Lawrence, Kansas. 80" × 80".

Susannah always follows her own muse, taking a printed pattern and running in a new direction. Her color emphasis is pinks and purples with a decided Japanese look, a palette reflected from the Japanese-style print used in the 1 1/2 " sawtooth border. Her quilting design is a vine sprouting flowers she drew from the blocks.

Susannah picked her nine favorite baskets and then drew her own setting blocks from four of the florals. Her blocks are an inch smaller than the patterns in the book. She redrafted them to 14". The quilted border is 9 1/2".

Florals

The fun with batiks is finding the perfect painterly print that looks just like the flower petals. You'll need at least
2 fat quarters, light and dark, of the following colors:

- yellow
- pink
- orange
- purple
- blue
- green
- red
- 3 extra fat quarters of green for the stems and leaves
- 1/2 yard piece for the optional stem in the sashing. You'll need to cut 16 yards of 1/2" finished bias.

Background

3 yards of a black batik with a very subtle hand-dyed look for the blocks.
If you want to sash the quilt with 3" sashing and add a 3" border of the same black buy 4 1/2 yards more.

Lotsa Dots by Deb Rowden, Lawrence, Kansas. Machine quilted by Lori Kukuk. 90" x 90". Deb Rowden is besotted with dots, so her challenge was finding enough dotted prints to make each block of different prints, a charm quilt of sorts. Her multi-colored quilt is quite charming. The unspoken color rule in the 1930s was "Any color goes with any color." Deb's reminded us that the rule holds true today.

The only fabric in this very modern version of the traditional basket sampler that isn't a dot is the stripe in the sashing. Deb decided to correct that omission by adding appliqued 2" circles at the sashing intersections. The border is 9" wide. See a similar quilt on page 150 for yardage and construction information and start buying dots.

Black & White & Re(a)d All Over by Joyce Colton, Lecompton, Kansas. 88" x 88". Machine quilted by Lori Kukuk. Joyce sashed the blocks with 2" strips of white that blended into the blocks. She added a 1 1/2" plaid border framed by a 6" outer border.

Fabric shops are full of potential. One needn't follow color rules to make a quilt that blends into the bedroom décor. When Joyce Colton began planning a model for the monthly *Star* blocks, she remembered her father's favorite joke.

"What's black and white and red all over? A newspaper!"

She decided those colors were perfect for a quilt made from newspaper patterns and combined a stack of reds with an impressive collection of black and white prints to make a striking quilt. The quilt - very 21st century - also calls to mind a retro kitchen with white-tiled walls and a pair of red vinyl upholstered chrome chairs.

Pam Mayfield's version of "Ruby's Swanky Basket" in warm tones of pink and brown is surrounded by McKim patterns and catalogs. The "Chinese Lantern Pods" is from McKim's "Flower Garden Series," a popular embroidery design for a sampler quilt. For a full view of Pam's *Designer Basket* sampler see page 165.

Ruby McKim
Needlework Trendsetter

Quilt pattern columns seem at home in the Kansas City area, possibly due to the innovations and influence of one woman. In 1916, twenty-five-year-old Ruby Short collaborated with children's author Thornton Burgess to produce a series of quilt patterns in *The Kansas City Star*. The *Bed-Time Quilt* featured embroidered animals from *Burgess* stories outlined in rather cubistic fashion, a style McKim called "Quaddy Quilties. McKim biographer Jill Sutton Filo has speculated the strange name is a possible reference to the quadrilateral shapes of the quadrupeds. In the early 1920s McKim's modern quilt blocks began appearing in other papers. The "Quaddy Quilties" in the *Bed-Time Quilt* are thought to be the first syndicated pattern series.

Ruby Short was born July 27, 1891, to Morris Trimble Short and Viola M. Vernon Short in Millersburg, Illinois. Morris was 47 at Ruby's birth, 24 years older than his wife. In 1899, the Shorts moved west to

Independence, Missouri, near Kansas City. Independence, an old river town, had once been a primary port for western migration and an outpost of Confederate sympathy during the Civil War. A branch of the Mormon Church, the Reorganized Latter Day Saints, had made the town their headquarters in the 1830s. The Shorts came to Independence because the town was the "center place" of their religion.

Ruby's Swanky Basket

orris Short died two years after their arrival, leaving Viola a widow at thirty-four with ten-year-old Ruby, a younger son named June and a daughter Cordie. Ruby's art talent was apparent even as a girl. Her adolescent drawings show the same sure hand and sense of style as her later needlework designs. Viola managed to send Ruby to art school for a time. She attended the New York School of Fine and Applied Arts (now Parsons School of Design) but did not graduate.

She returned to Independence and became a public school art teacher. Ruby soon took a position at a trade school in the Kansas City school system. While teaching, Ruby published the "Quaddie Quiltie Bed-Time Quilt." In 1917 she married Arthur McKim, whom she'd known since childhood.

In the early 1920s, they founded McKim Studios. Arthur was in charge of the business and editorial departments, while Ruby did the designing. They syndicated quilt and needlework patterns, published pattern booklets and mail-order catalogs, and sold kits under the name McKim-Cut Quilts, while raising two girls and a boy. Quilt design, with its inexpensive patterns, was a good business when women had little to spend on their hobbies, and McKim Studios, one of the earliest of the quilt cottage industries, was quite successful.

(Continued, Page 27)

Rotary Cutting the Basket

Piece J: Cut one 15 7/8" square of background fabric. Cut it in half diagonally to make two triangles. Save one for another block. Appliqué the bouquet to one triangle. (There is no template for piece J)

Piece K: Cut two 3" by 10-7/8" rectangles of background fabric. Trim the 45 degree angles or use the template.

Piece L: Cut four 3 3/8" squares of dark blue and one of light blue. Cut each in half diagonally to make two triangles. You need eight dark triangles and two light.

Piece M: Cut three 5 7/8" squares: one of light blue, one of dark blue and one of background. Cut each in half diagonally to make triangles. You'll need one of each.

Piecing the Basket

Pattern testers think it's best to piece the whole basket block and then do the appliqué. To do this, leave a little space unstitched between piece J and the bottom half of the basket for the appliquéd stem. After the basket is pieced, appliqué the flower. Tuck the stem in the space and stitch the hole closed.

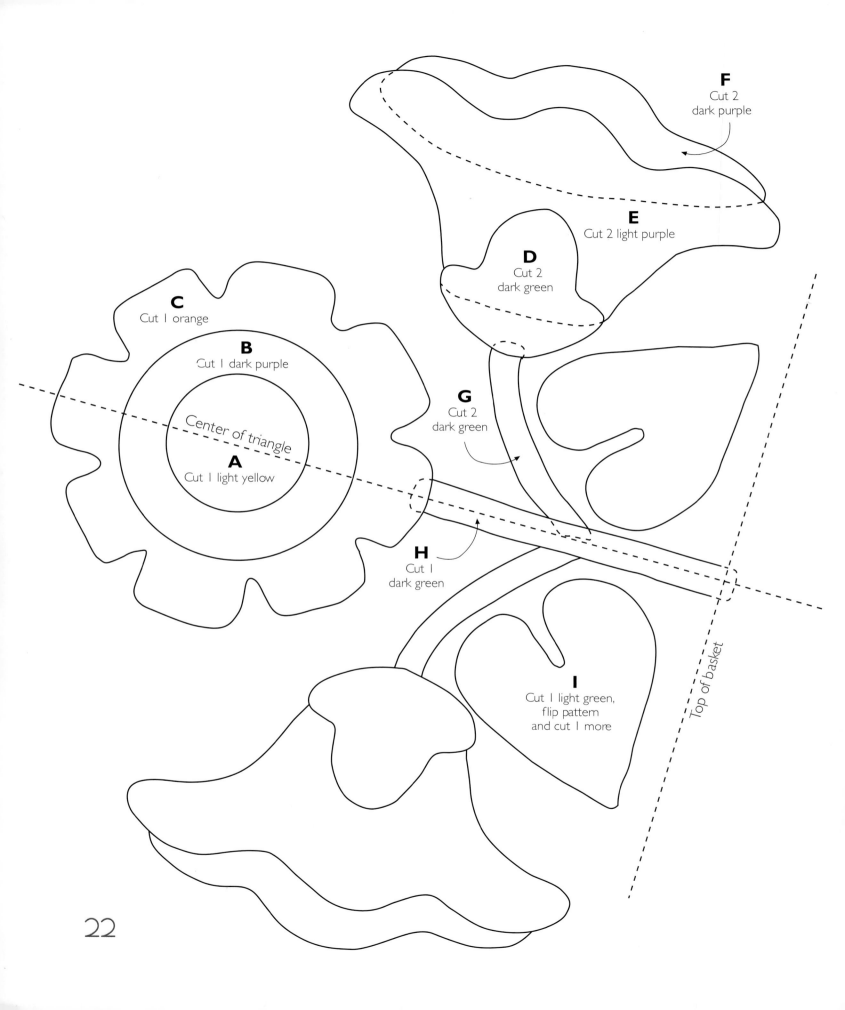

F
Cut 2
dark purple

E
Cut 2 light purple

D
Cut 2
dark green

C
Cut 1 orange

B
Cut 1 dark purple

Center of triangle

A
Cut 1 light yellow

G
Cut 2
dark green

H
Cut 1
dark green

I
Cut 1 light green,
flip pattern
and cut 1 more

Top of basket

Illus. 1.11b

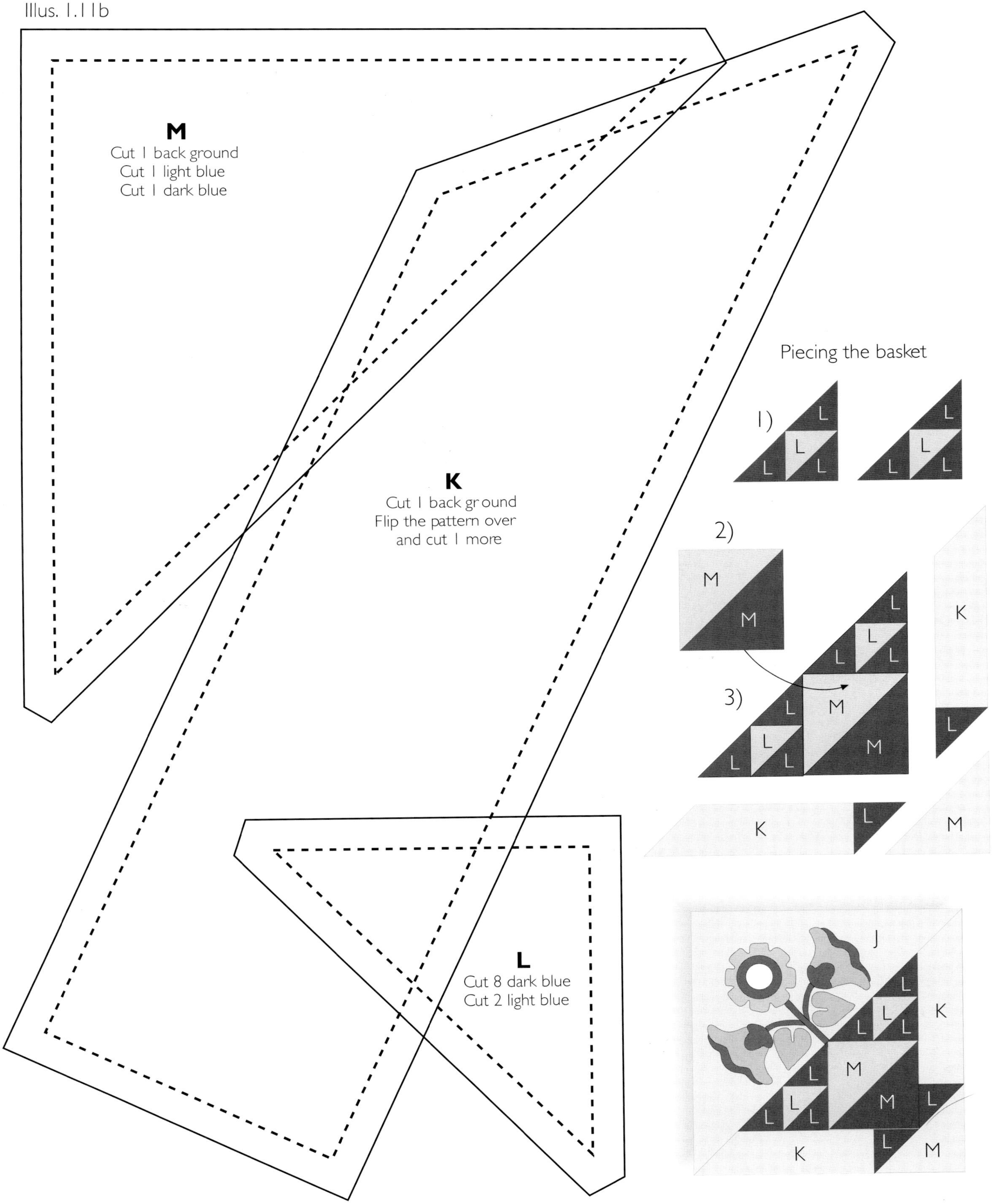
M
Cut 1 back ground
Cut 1 light blue
Cut 1 dark blue
K
Cut 1 back ground
Flip the pattern over
and cut 1 more
L
Cut 8 dark blue
Cut 2 light blue
Piecing the basket
1)
2)
3)
L
M
K
J

Swanky Table Runner

The table runner was inspired by Ruby McKim's pillow designs.
Her "swanky oil cloth pillows" seemed a good match for Barbara's
collection of black and white dishes, both antique and reproduction.

Swanky Table Runner

16-1/2" x 41-1/2"

Try the pattern with any of the flowers from the basket sampler. They'll all fit into the circular bowl. See page 25 for the floral templates. The appliquéd bowl is based on an old 45 record. Every quilter should have a 33 - 1/3, a 45 and a CD among her sewing tools for a range of circular templates. The holes in the center help with placement.

Fabric Requirements

- 1/2 yard of black check for the background
- 1/2 yard of backing fabric
- 1 fat quarter of black and white checkerboard for the basket
- Scraps of light and dark purples, light and dark orange and light and medium green for the floral

Cutting

The Blocks

- Wash the background fabric, trim the selvages and square the edges so you have a rectangle about 17" x 42".
- Cut the appliqué pieces as indicated on the templates, adding a bit less than 1/4" for seam allowances.

Stitching

- Press the background in half the long way to create a crease down the center to use as a placement line.
- Place the bowls two inches from the ends.
- Place the floral appliqué and glue, baste or pin the pieces in place.
- Stitch using your favorite appliqué method.
- Press.

Finishing

- Trim the backing fabric the same size as the top.
- Place the two pieces face sides together and stitch around the edges as shown leaving a place to turn the runner.
- Cut excess from corners.
- Turn the runner inside out and press.
- Finish the edges of the hole by hand or machine.

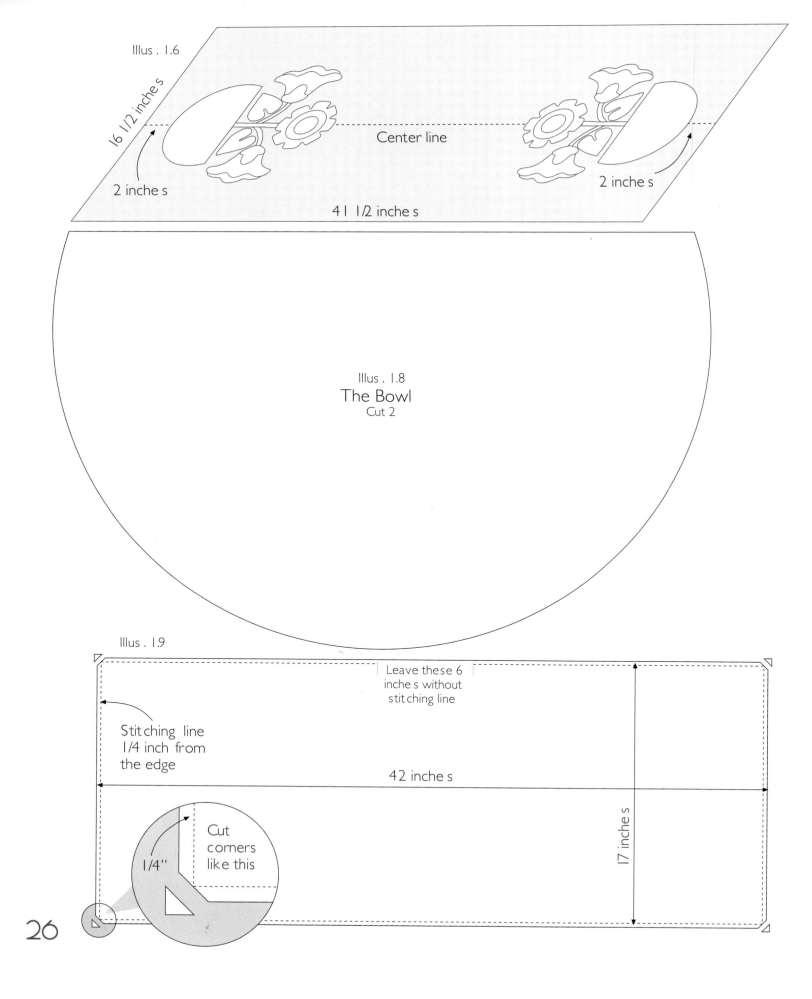

Illus . 1.6

16 1/2 inches

2 inches

Center line

2 inches

41 1/2 inches

Illus . 1.8
The Bowl
Cut 2

Illus . 1.9

Leave these 6 inches without stitching line

Stitching line 1/4 inch from the edge

42 inches

17 inches

1/4"

Cut corners like this

(Continued from Page 21)

Son Kim recalled a warm home in which all the beds "boasted a handmade quilt as the top cover." Quilts, both antique and those made in Ruby's designs, were stored in "heaping stacks," in a "big hall closet." Ruby's murals of the family at work and play covered the walls of their house in Independence.

In September, 1928, Ruby launched a new series in *The Kansas City Star*. "The Pine Tree Quilt," a traditional design, was the first of over 1,000 full-sized patterns the newspaper would print in the next three decades. She designed the weekly quilt block for *The Star* until 1930, when Eveline Foland took over the column. Ruby's patterns were syndicated to numerous other newspapers around the country. She also wrote and designed for magazines such as *Better Homes and Gardens*, *Child Life*, and *Successful Farming*.

Most of her creative work in quilt design was finished by the time she was forty. Husband and wife decided to take their children on a trip to Europe in 1933, during the depths of the Depression when money for most families was in short supply. The quilt pattern business had been a good career choice for the McKims.

During the early 1930s, Ruby's attention turned to antique dolls. She was editor of Doll Talk magazine for decades and the family business evolved into Kimport Dolls. Arthur died in June, 1967 at 76, and Ruby followed in July, 1976, a few days short of her 85th birthday.

The pieced design in "Ruby's Swanky Basket" is drawn from one called "Grape Basket" that appeared with a McKim Studios signature in March, 1930. The bouquet was inspired by a design advertised in her needlework catalogs under the headline "Swanky Oil Cloth Pillows." The copy noted the pillows were purely decorative: "These colorful pillows are for sheer swank and gayety; not even the cat could bury himself on their slippery sides!"

SWANKY OIL CLOTH PILLOWS

McKim's use of black backgrounds was a color scheme favored more for home decoration than for quilts.

Kathy Delaney's quilt uses reproduction prints and plains to capture the look of the classic '30s quilt. See page 147 for the full quilt.

Pale green was the height of fashion for interior design and quilts at the time. We sometimes call it "Kitchen Green" because so many kitchens were painted and decorated in the shade, but the Sears, Roebuck & Co. catalogs of the era called it Nile Green. Ditsy flowers in Nile Green prints, an old pincushion and a sewing kit with Barbara's mother's purple darning egg complement original Foland designs - blocks from her *Memory Bouquet* quilt and her stylized *Sunbonnet Sue* pattern from a 1930 *Kansas City Star*.

Eveline Foland
Mystery Designer

Eveline Foland's graceful drawings appeared in *The Kansas City Star* over her bold signature from March, 1929 through 1932. At first, Foland's quilt patterns alternated with designs by Ruby McKim, but soon Foland conducted the column on her own, drawing about 130 designs. Most were her illustrations of traditional quilts shared by readers. She also designed several of her own modern patterns, inspired by contemporary taste. The flower in "Eveline's Posey" (that's the way she spelled posey) reflects both the simple shapes of modernism and the graceful lines of art nouveau, characteristics of her distinctive style.

Eveline Alice Smith was born January 22, 1893 in Kansas City, daughter of Canadians Elliot F. and Lily L. Whitelaw Smith. Quilt pattern historian Wilene Smith has found much about Eveline's early life, and published information in the *Baldwin* (Kansas) *Ledger* February 28, 1985. Eveline was the youngest of three children. She

graduated from Kansas City's Central High School in 1908 and spent a year at the Kansas City Art Institute in 1910. Eveline (pattern collectors pronounce her name Eh - vah - leen') taught at the Jane Hayes Gates School, later incorporated into Manual High School. The school offered courses for women over 14 years of age, teaching them the trades of dressmaking, millinery, factory sewing and commercial art.

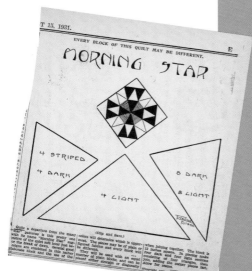

"Morning Star" with Foland's high-style lettering appeared in August, 1931.

Eveline's Posey

Rotary Cutting the Basket

Piece G: Cut one 15 7/8" square of background fabric. Cut it in half diagonally to make two triangles. Appliqué the posey to one triangle. Save the other for another block. (There is no template for G)

Piece H: Cut four light yellow 3" squares and two dark yellow.

Piece I: Cut three 3 3/8" squares of dark yellow. Cut each in half diagonally to make two triangles. You need six dark triangles.

Piece J: Cut two rectangles, 3" by 10 7/8" of background and trim the 45-degree angle on the ends. It may be easier to use the template.

Piece K: Cut one 5 7/8" square of background. Cut it in half diagonally to make two triangles. You'll only need one, so save the other for another block.

Piecing the Basket

As with the first block, piece the whole basket block and then do the appliqué. To do this, leave a little space unstitched between piece G between and the basket for the appliquéd stem. After the basket is pieced, appliqué the flower. Tuck the stem in the space and stitch the hole closed.

Eveline Foland

She married a salesman, James E. Foland, in 1922 and they adopted a boy, James Elliot Foland, about 1925. She began illustrating *Star* fashion and home decoration features about the same time. She and Foland divorced in 1931. Quilt historians lose track of Eveline Foland in 1933 after her last pattern appeared in *The Kansas City Star*. For a while, she continued free - lance fashion illustration in Kansas City. She probably remarried, changed her name and moved from the area, making her difficult to find in public records, especially during the Depression when city directories and phone books were rather sparse. Her later life remains a mystery.

Baskets and bouquets may be traditional quilt design of grandmother's day, but Foland's versions have the look of the modern age. Her checked basket pattern was published as "Grandmother's Basket" in *The Kansas City Star* in February, 1932. The appliquéd flower is a detail from her updated 1930 "Sunbonnet Sue."

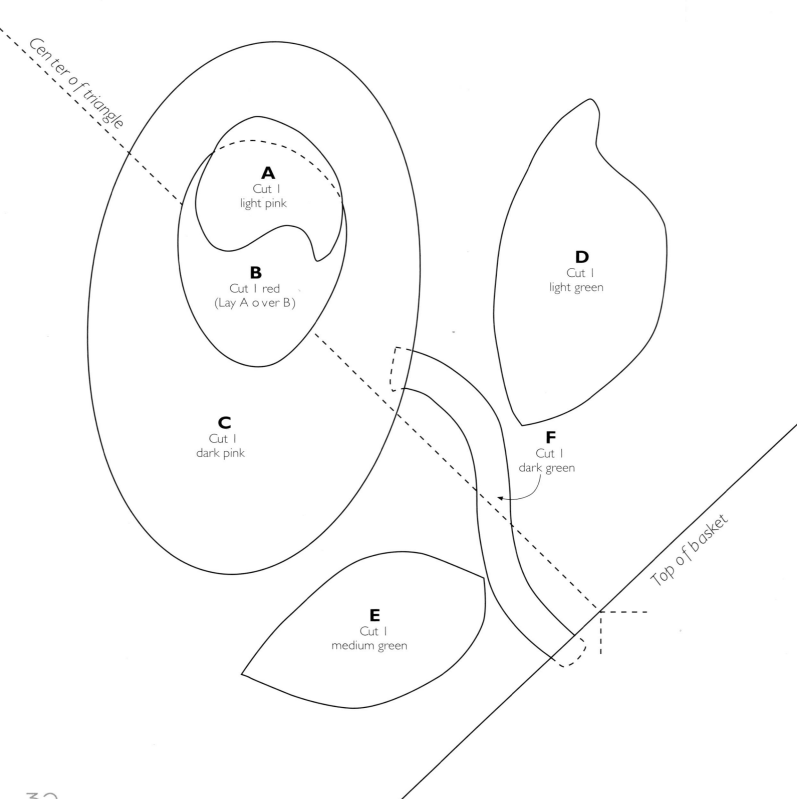

Center of triangle

A
Cut 1
light pink

B
Cut 1 red
(Lay A over B)

C
Cut 1
dark pink

D
Cut 1
light green

F
Cut 1
dark green

E
Cut 1
medium green

Top of basket

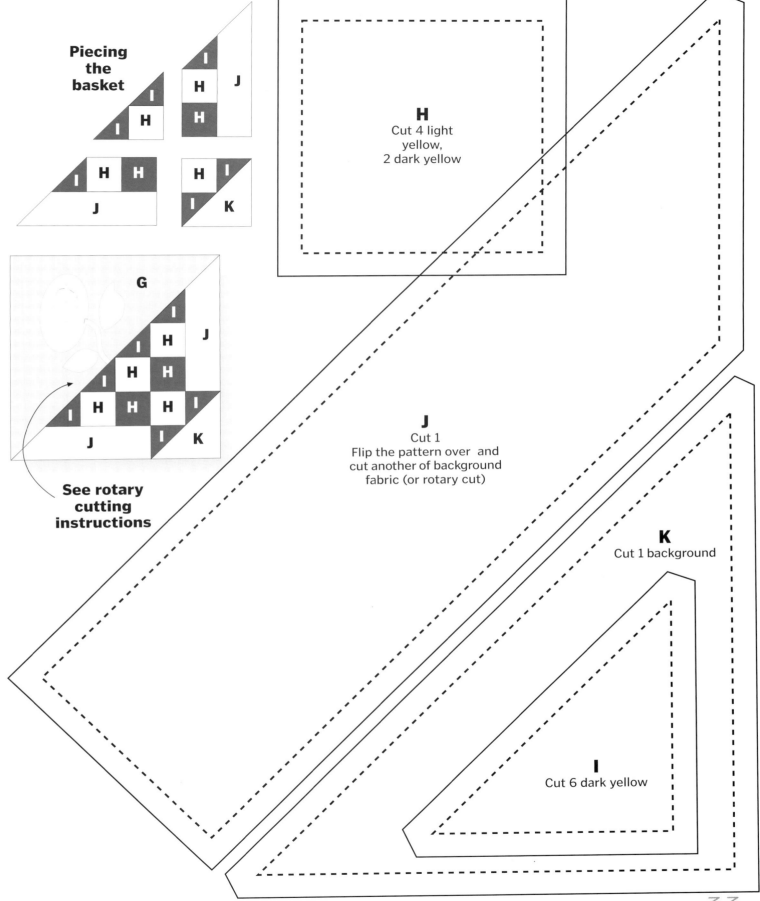

Piecing the basket

H
Cut 4 light yellow,
2 dark yellow

See rotary cutting instructions

J
Cut 1
Flip the pattern over and cut another of background fabric (or rotary cut)

K
Cut 1 background

I
Cut 6 dark yellow

33

You can adapt other florals in the Designer Basket to make this repeating block baby quilt. The Morning Glory (Basket #3), the Pansy (Basket #5) and the Orchid (Basket #8) will fit into a 10'' finished block. Just trim the stem with a diagonal cut, the same way florists cut a flower from the garden.

Posey Baby Quilt

On the chair is the *Posey Baby Quilt* by Barbara Brackman, Lawrence, Kansas. Hand appliquéd and hand quilted. 40'' x 40''.

Barbara's small quilt, photographed while still in the quilting stage, echoes the shades of the old Log Cabin quilt folded on the wicker chair.

Posey Baby Quilt

40" x 40"

10" Blocks

You'll Need:

9 Appliquéd Blocks finishing to 10"
Check Sashing & Border finishing to 2-1/2"
wide

Fabric Requirements

The Blocks

Barbara used scraps left over from the
Designer Basket sampler. She'd collected light,
medium and dark versions of the muted
shades popular today. The prints are
monochromatic—figure and ground in each
print are variations of the same hue. If you
want to buy fabric specifically for this quilt buy
fat quarters (18" x 22" cuts) of the following:
- 2 light pinks, 2 medium, 2 dark
- 2 light purples, 2 medium, 2 dark
- 1 light orange, 1 medium, 1 dark
- 2 light yellows, 2 medium, 2 dark
- 2 light blues, 2 medium, 2 dark
- 1 medium green for the leaves & stems

The Sashing & Border

- 1/2 yard light green
- 1/2 yard dark purple + an extra 1/2 yard for binding

"Eveline's Posey," drawn from a detail in
Eveline Foland's 1930 Sunbonnet Sue design,
makes a sweet baby quilt in today's updated
pastel shades. The appliqué is easy enough for
a beginner and quick enough for the quilter
with a nine-month deadline who's let too
many months slip by.

The flower is an abstraction composed of
basic shapes, a floral style that was quite
popular in mid-century design. Today's fabric
designers call simple floral prints ditsies, a
word that seems to mean a nondescript
flower that really isn't recognizable as anything
found in nature. During the 1925-1950 time
period, designers loved ditsies for both cotton
prints and appliqué design.

Backing

- I 1/4 yards will make a 42" square backing you don't have to piece together.

Cutting:

The Blocks

- Cut 9 squares 10-1/2" for backgrounds.
- Cut the appliqué templates as indicated on the pieces, adding a bit less than 1/4" for seam allowances.

The Sashing & Border

- Cut 56 squares 3" of light fabric.
- Cut 55 squares 3" of dark.

Stitching the Blocks

For information about books that teach hand and machine appliqué see page 8.

- Prepare the appliqué pieces using your favorite method.
- Press the backgrounds to create horizontal, vertical and diagonal creases for placement.
- Glue, baste or pin the pieces in place using the guidelines on the pattern.
- Stitch the pieces down using your favorite technique.

Setting the Quilt

- Piece vertical sashing strips by alternating dark and light squares to make checked strips of 4 squares each.
- Piece longer horizontal strips by alternating dark and light squares to make 4 checked strips of 16 squares each.
- Position these strips on your design wall so the dark and light squares fall in the correct places.
- Alternate vertical sashing strips with the blocks as shown to make 3 strips of 3 blocks and 4 sashing strips, as shown.
- Add the horizontal checked strips as shown in the finished quilt.

Quilting

Barbara hand quilted the blocks by quilting 1/4" lines inside the ovals in the flower and stitching a line down the middle of each leaf and stem. She echoed the flower's shape in lines about 3/4" apart. In the checked sashing she drew a leaf inspired by a design popular with today's machine quilters.

Illus . 2.7

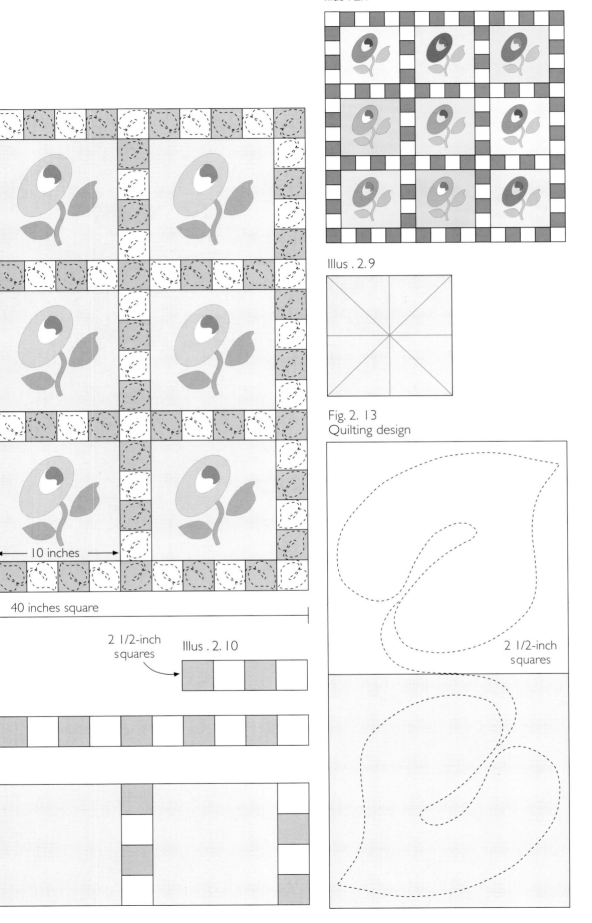

Illus . 2.8

10 inches

40 inches square

2 1/2-inch squares

Illus . 2.10

Illus . 2.11

Illus . 2.12

Illus . 2.9

Fig. 2. 13
Quilting design

2 1/2-inch squares

Edna Marie Dunn's fashion illustrations and a gift book show the range of her design ideas. Underneath, Denise Mariano's hand-quilted block captures the brilliance of a morning glory in the abstract prints today's quilters call batiks. See page 166 for another view of *Garden of Joy*.

Edna Marie Dunn
The Star's Fashion Illustrator

In 1932, a new signature appeared in *The Kansas City Star*'s quilt pattern column. The Star's fashion illustrator, Edna Marie Dunn, took over the column after Eveline Foland's departure. Dunn signed only four of her early patterns, but she was the feature's anonymous editor for the next three decades. Between 1932 and 1961, Dunn edited and drew the hundreds of quilt patterns printed in *The Star*.

Dunn asked readers throughout the subscription area to send in favorite designs. Each week she drafted the patterns with her T-square and ruler, printing the suggested name and crediting the contributor. If the pattern was unnamed, Dunn did some quick research to find a name or made one up herself. She told Louise Townsend, who interviewed her in 1978, that, "she was too busy with her fashion illustration work to spend much time researching quilt names or designing patterns."

Over the years, her quilt illustrations seem to reflect the time she had to devote to the drawing. The earlier designs have some of the flair that McKim and Foland added to the feature, but as the decades went by, style and space were minimal.

Edna Marie Dunn (1893-1983) was born in Chicago and moved to Kansas City as a child. She graduated from Christian College in Columbia, Missouri, and attended the Chicago Academy of Art. She returned to Kansas City, illustrating fashion for department stores such as Harzfeld's, Woolf Brothers and Rothschild's. In 1922, Dunn won a competition to become a fashion artist for *The Kansas City Star*.

Edna's Morning Glory

Her niece Shirley Mikesell recalled her method of working. Each Monday she visited the department stores, making quick sketches of featured garments. Over the week she finished black-and-white washes that appeared in *The Star* day by day in the following week. "These preliminary sketches amaze the novice," wrote Shirley. "From two or three flowing lines, a dart or button indicated, one flower to signify an allover print, she could produce from memory a detailed front and rear-view drawing." Unlike most of her quilt patterns, her fashion illustrations were always signed.

Edna Marie Dunn taught many of Kansas City's aspiring artists at her own school at 3820 Main Street, the Edna Marie Dunn School of Fashion, which she began in 1938. She and her husband Frank E. Douglass also operated a stationery business that published cards and gift books in Edna's designs. When Frank died in 1964, she retired. Edna lived to be 90.

Dunn rarely designed a pattern herself, but the "Morning Glory" seems to be one of her originals, published in a signed column in December, 1933. Intended to be a small embroidery design, the flower makes a delightful appliqué. The basket with its pieced handle is adapted from a "Hanging Basket" published in August, 1937.

Rotary Cutting the Basket

Piece I: Cut one 10 7/8" square of dark and one 10 7/8" square of light fabric. Cut each in half diagonally to make two triangles. Save the other piece for another block. (There is no template for I.)

Piece J: Cut one 3" square of dark fabric.

Piece K: Cut five 3 3/8" squares of dark fabric and five 3 3/8" squares of background fabric. Cut each in half diagonally to make two triangles so you'll have 10 dark triangles and 10 background.

Piece L: Cut two 3" by 10 7/8" rectangles of background and trim the 45 degree angle on the ends. It may be easier to use the template.

Piece M: Cut one 5 7/8" square of background fabric. Cut it in half diagonally to make two triangles. You'll only need one, so save the other for another block.

Piecing the Basket

Piece the whole basket block and then do the appliqué. To do this, leave a little space unstitched between the two "I" pieces for the appliquéd stem. After the basket is pieced, appliqué the flower. Tuck the stem in the space and stitch the hole closed.

41

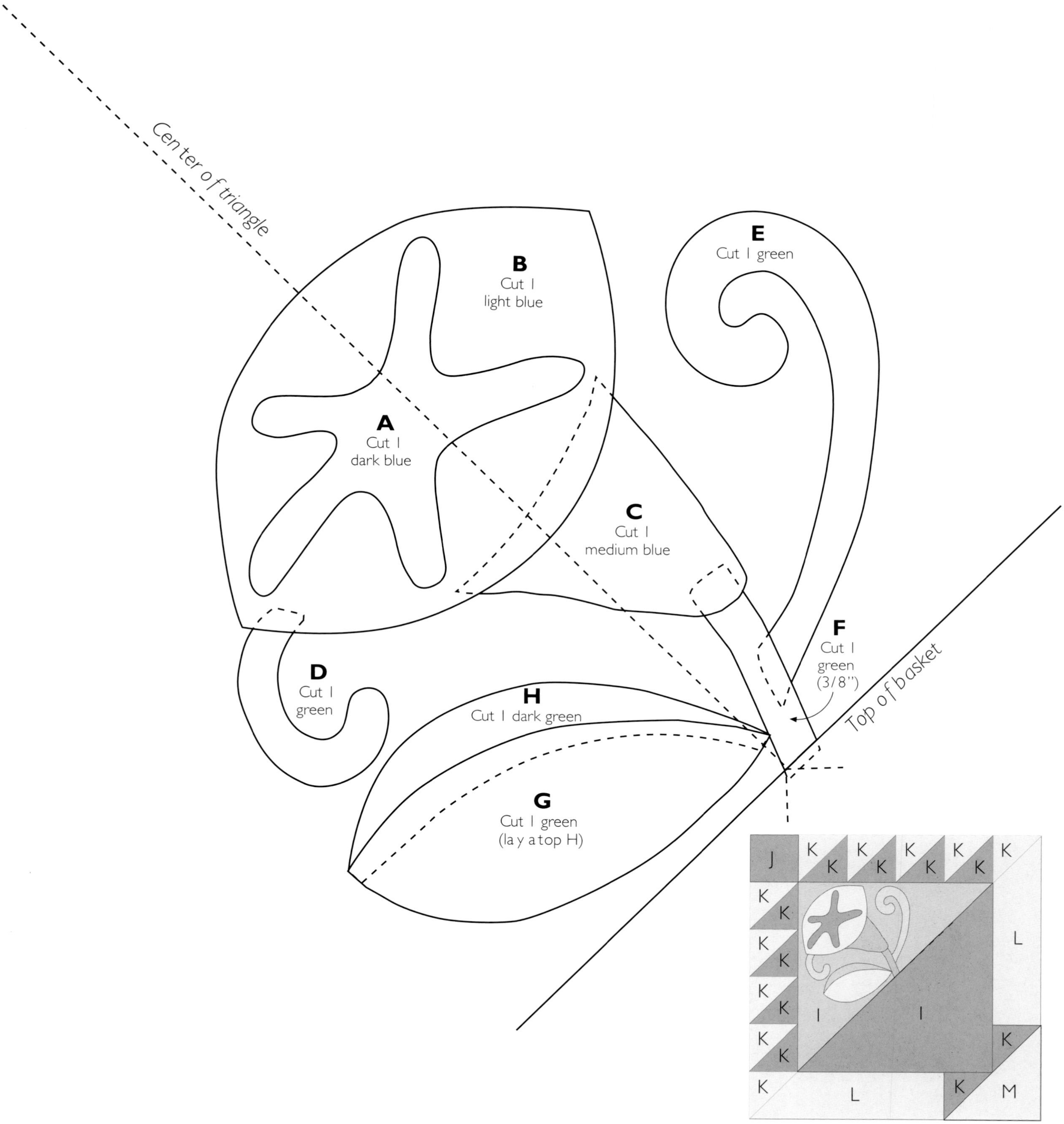
Center of triangle
A
Cut 1
dark blue
B
Cut 1
light blue
C
Cut 1
medium blue
D
Cut 1
green
E
Cut 1 green
F
Cut 1
green
(3/8")
G
Cut 1 green
(lay atop H)
H
Cut 1 dark green
Top of basket
J
K
L
I
M

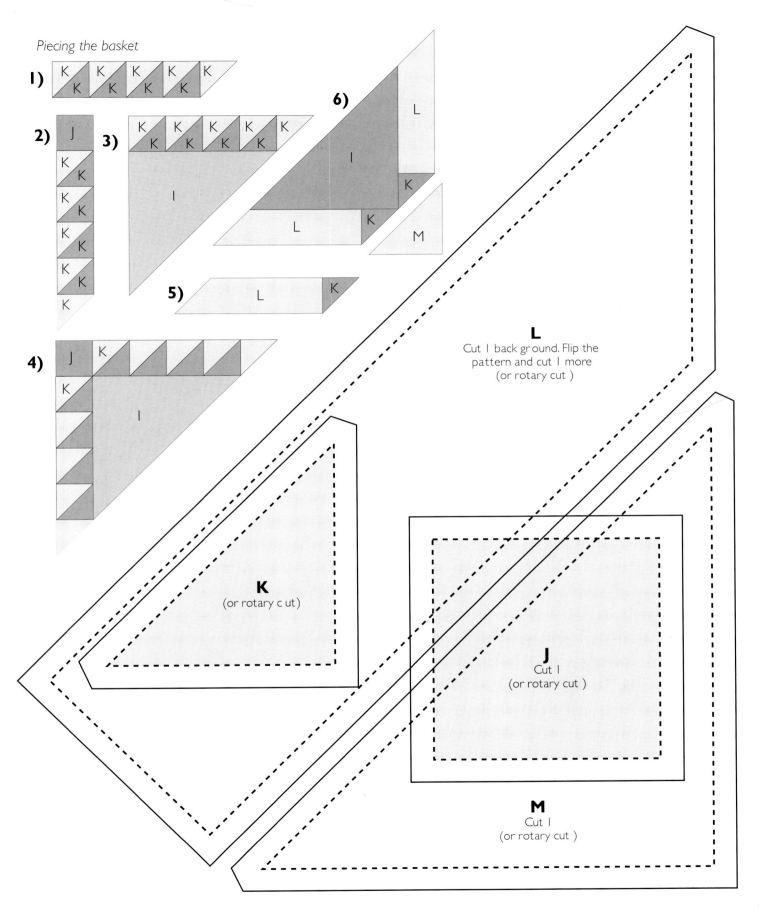

Piecing the basket

1) K K K K K

2) J

3) I

4) J K I

5) L K

6) L I K L K M

L
Cut 1 back ground. Flip the
pattern and cut 1 more
(or rotary cut)

K
(or rotary c ut)

J
Cut 1
(or rotary cut)

M
Cut 1
(or rotary cut)

43

Joyce Colton's striking version of "Aunt Martha's Checked Basket" is shown
with a catalog advertising dress prints of "standard quality," the cottons used in
quilts, for 8-1/2 cents per yard. Above that catalog is a reproduction print
from *The Star's Patterns of History* fabric collection. The green booklet features
patterns from one of the quilt block contests that Colonial Patterns held in
the 1930s. Aunt Martha herself is pictured admiring a modern prizewinner.
See a photo of Joyce's *Black and White and Re(a)d All Over* quilt on page 2.

44

Aunt Martha
Colonial Persona

Aunt Martha is a fictional character who represents a long-time Kansas City needlework company, Colonial Patterns. In the days of the Great Depression, Clara and Jack Tillotson recognized that quilts might be a good business. Their first idea was selling Clara's handmade quilts, but people hadn't the money for such extravagance. The Tillotsons then created the Colonial Readicut Quilt Block Company, a cottage industry specializing in quilt patches cut to the correct size and shape. Again, kits were too costly during the hard times, so they added paper patterns to their line. At a dime a piece, the patterns were affordable and quite popular during the 1930s quilt craze. In a 1980 interview, Jack Tillotson recalled his best customers, who wrote to "say they weren't going to buy another pattern, that they had suit boxes full of them under the bed." Despite such protests, another coin would soon arrive in an order.

The Tillotsons began advertising their designs around the country in newspapers and magazines. The ads looked like a regular newspaper column, with a little quilt lore and instructions about buying a pattern or booklet through the mail.

The name Aunt Martha became their signature after a Chicago editor decided the feature needed a grandmotherly name with the right touch of Colonial history. The Colonial Pattern Company's nom-de-plume reminded readers of both Martha Washington and everybody's quiltmaking aunt.

Clara Tillotson knew quite a bit about quilts, but as demand for the patterns grew, she and her husband expanded their knowledge by visiting libraries to search for antique patterns in the few books available. They sketched quilt designs at county fairs and they sponsored contests asking customers to mail quilt blocks made up in their favorite designs.

They also hired professional designers, among them Marguerite Weaver, who'd been a student of *Kansas City Star* designer Eveline Foland. In a 1980 interview, Marguerite

45

Aunt Martha's Checkered Basket

recalled that her specialty was embroidered pillow slips and finger towels, but she also designed original patchwork. By 1936, when she was hired, the company's focus was no longer reproducing old-fashioned designs, but creating novel variations of the classics.

The company occasionally gathered a group of single patterns into packets called *Aunt Martha's Work Basket*, an idea that developed into a monthly magazine named *The Work Basket*, containing patterns for all kinds of needle-work. (For more about *Work Basket*, see the next section.)

In 1949, the Tillotsons sold the Aunt Martha arm of the company to Mr. and Mrs. Clifford Swenson. Aunt Martha's Studio changed its name back to Colonial Patterns in 1974 when Edward C. Price II purchased the pattern company. Colonial Patterns, Inc. currently sells several Aunt Martha's booklets with full-size patchwork and quilting patterns.

"Aunt Martha's Checked Basket" combines two designs mailed by fans of Aunt Martha who entered their pattern contests in the 1930s. The basket, which is rather complicated due to the extra strip along the bottom, was sent by Mrs. J. O. Royce of Indiana. The flower was drawn from a design by Mrs. Byron Cooper of Coffeyville, Kansas.

This envelope contains a single printed sheet, rather extravagant pattern packaging for the time.

Rotary Cutting the Basket

Piece I: Cut one 15 7/8-inch square of background fabric. Cut each in half diagonally to make two triangles. You'll need one.

Piece J: Cut two 3 1/2-inch light green squares and one dark green. Cut each in half diagonally to make triangles. You'll need three light triangles and two dark.

Piece K: Cut one 3 1/8-inch light square and two dark 3 1/8-inch squares.

Piece L: Cut two strips, 9 5/8" by 4 1/8" of background fabric. Trim one end of each at a 45-degree angle or use the template.

Piece M: Cut one strip, 1 1/4-inches by 10", of light fabric. Trim one end of each at a 45-degree angle or use the template.

Piece N: Cut one square of background fabric 7" square. Cut in half diagonally to make two triangles. You'll need only one triangle. (There are no templates for I, J, or K.)

Piecing the Basket

Pattern testers think it's best to piece the whole basket block and then do the appliqué. To do this, leave a little space unstitched between pieces I and J for the appliquéd stem. After the basket is pieced, appliqué the flower. Tuck the stem in the space and stitch the hole closed.

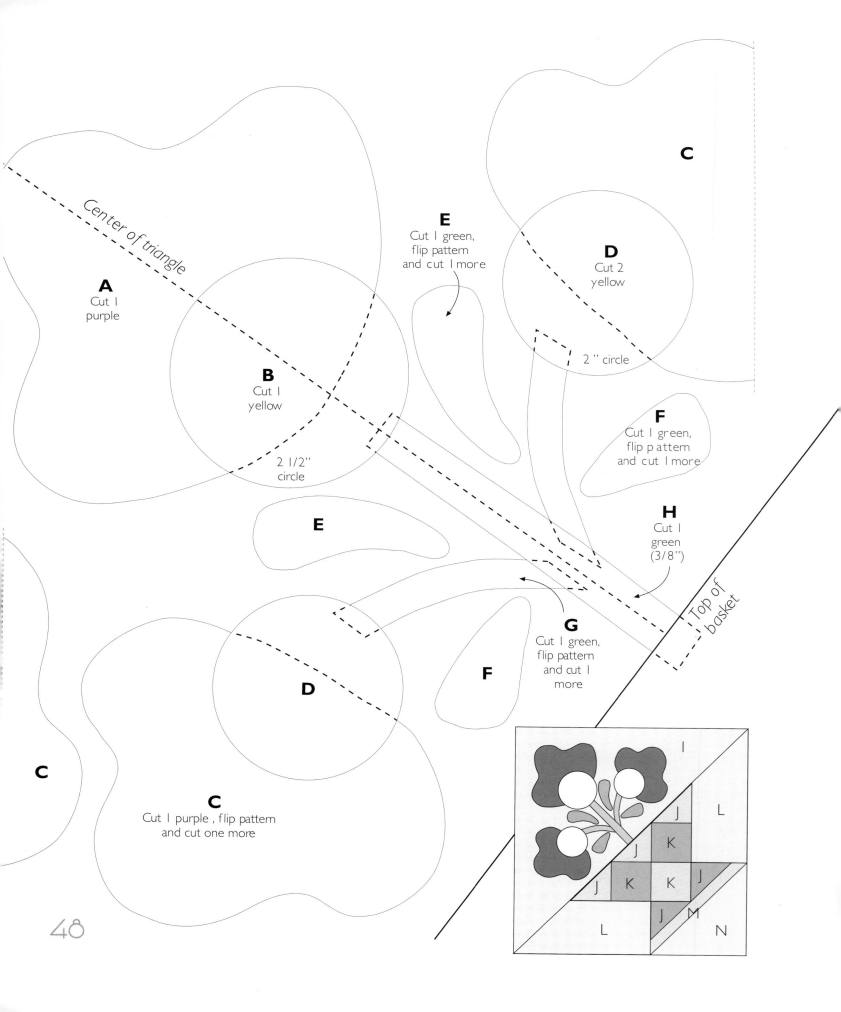

Center of triangle

A
Cut 1
purple

E
Cut 1 green,
flip pattern
and cut 1 more

D
Cut 2
yellow

C

B
Cut 1
yellow

2 1/2"
circle

2 " circle

F
Cut 1 green,
flip pattern
and cut 1 more

E

H
Cut 1
green
(3/8")

Top of basket

G
Cut 1 green,
flip pattern
and cut 1
more

F

D

C

C
Cut 1 purple , flip pattern
and cut one more

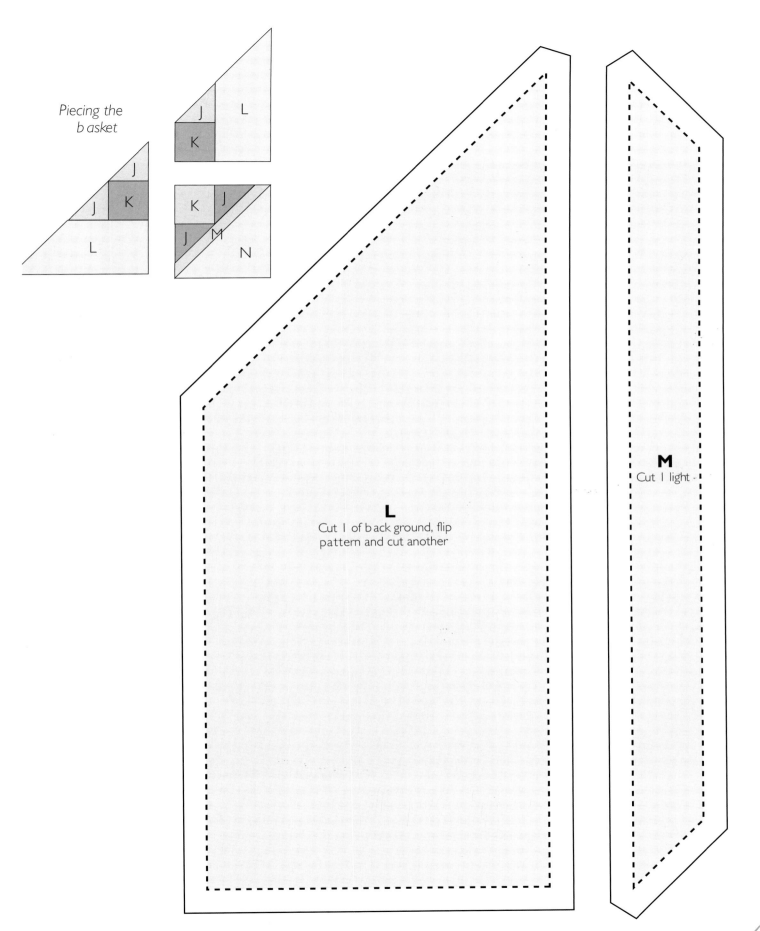

Piecing the basket

J
L
K

J
J K
L

K J
J M
N

L
Cut 1 of background, flip
pattern and cut another

M
Cut 1 light

49

Lattice Fan

Lattice Fan, by Jean Pearson Stanclift and Barbara Brackman, Lawrence, Kansas. Machine quilted by Lori Kukuk. 42" x 42". During the 1930s quilters loved to contrast plains and prints. We've updated the colors here by adopting a more recent design idea, high contrast between darks and lights of the same shade.

Lattice Fan

42" x 42"
8-1/2" Blocks

You'll Need:

16 Blocks finishing to 8-1/2"
4-inch border

This fan quilt is typical of Aunt Martha's mid-century patterns, traditional patchwork with a modern look, thanks to sophisticated ideas like the checkerboard coloring. Her original 1941 pattern featured curves in the lattice work, which were fine for hand-piecing. Here the pattern is modified so the arcs are replaced with straight lines perfect for machine-piecing over a paper foundation. We also give you templates if you prefer traditional piecing.

Fabric Requirements

The Blocks:

4 fat quarters (18 x 22") of 4 different black prints. Choose subtle black prints for texture.

(If you are appliquéing the backgrounds you need to get three 9" squares out of these fat quarters. Be sure you are going to have enough fabric after you wash and shrink the fat quarters. If not, buy 1/3 yard pieces.)

Barbara and Jean used scraps from the "Designer Basket" sampler and made 16 packets of light and dark shades of 16 different hues for the fans, a total of 32 different prints, half light and half dark. The prints are monochromatic, two or three shades of the same hue. If you are buying fabric you can get by with 16 fat quarters if you duplicate the color scheme in the fans. Buy pairs of light and dark prints of the following 8 colors:

- Pink
- Green
- Blue
- Purple
- Yellow
- Orange
- Aqua
- Raspberry

An alternate color scheme follows mid-century style by contrasting pastel prints and plains in the fan spokes. Use a slightly off-white plain for the background or update the look with a white on white print. This quilt would also be quite dramatic if the fans alternated black and white pieces in a checkerboard and the backgrounds were various pastels.

The Border:

- 1-1/4 yards of a subtle black print (you can also get 4 backgrounds from this print to total 5 different background prints in all.)

The Backing:

- 42" is just a bit to wide to squeeze a backing out of the width of today's fabric, so buy 1 3/4 yards and piece the backing.

Cutting

The Blocks:

- Decide how you want to piece this quilt. We give you several options.
- If you want to machine piece the fan spokes over paper foundations, you do not need to do any preliminary cutting of the checkerboard fans. See the foundations on page 56.

- If you want to do traditional piecing, either hand or machine, cut the fabrics using the templates as indicated for pieces C, D and E on page 54.
- You may want to piece the fans into curved background pieces. If so, cut fabrics for pieces A & B as indicated on the templates on page 54.
- You might prefer to appliqué the pieced fans onto the background, the method Jean chose for the quilt in the photo. If so, cut 16 9" background squares from the various black fabrics and ignore the templates for A & B.

The Border:

- Cut 2 strips 4-1/2" by 34-1/2" for the side borders.
- Cut 2 strips 4-1/2" by 42-1/2" for the top and bottom.

Stitching the Blocks

Paper Piecing the Fan Spokes over Paper Templates

- Photocopy the paper templates 16 times so you have 5 spokes for each of the 16 blocks. (4.8)
- Trim the foundations by leaving a 1/4"seam allowance around each.
- Beginning with piece 1, add the fabric to the back of the paper foundations as shown, making 5 spokes per fan. (4.9)
- Before removing the paper, seam the 5 spokes together.
- Add the background pieces and remove the paper when the blocks are finished.

Piecing the Fan Spokes in Traditional Methods

- Piece C, D & E into 5 spokes per fan block.
- Seam the spokes together.

Piecing the Fans into Arcs.

- Add pieces A and B as shown by piecing the curved seams. (4.10)

Appliquéing the Fans onto the Background.

- Turn the edges of the fan blocks under 1/4" and secure with basting, glue or pins.
- Position the fans onto the black backgrounds (4.11)
- Stitch using your favorite appliqué technique.

Setting the Quilt

- Press the fan blocks and trim to measure 9"
- Piece 4 strips of 4 blocks each.
- Piece the strips together as shown in the photograph.
- Press the top and trim edges to measure 34-1/2"
- Add the side borders.
- Add the top and bottom borders.

Quilting

Lori machine-quilted two straight lines in each spoke, and stitched along the long seam lines. She quilted a meandering line in the background of the blocks and a fan in the border. (4.12) Hand quilters might want to stitch similar designs or quilt a line 1/4" inside each of the seams of each piece to give the quilt a mid-century look. See 4.13 for a fan quilting design for the border.

Illus . 4.6

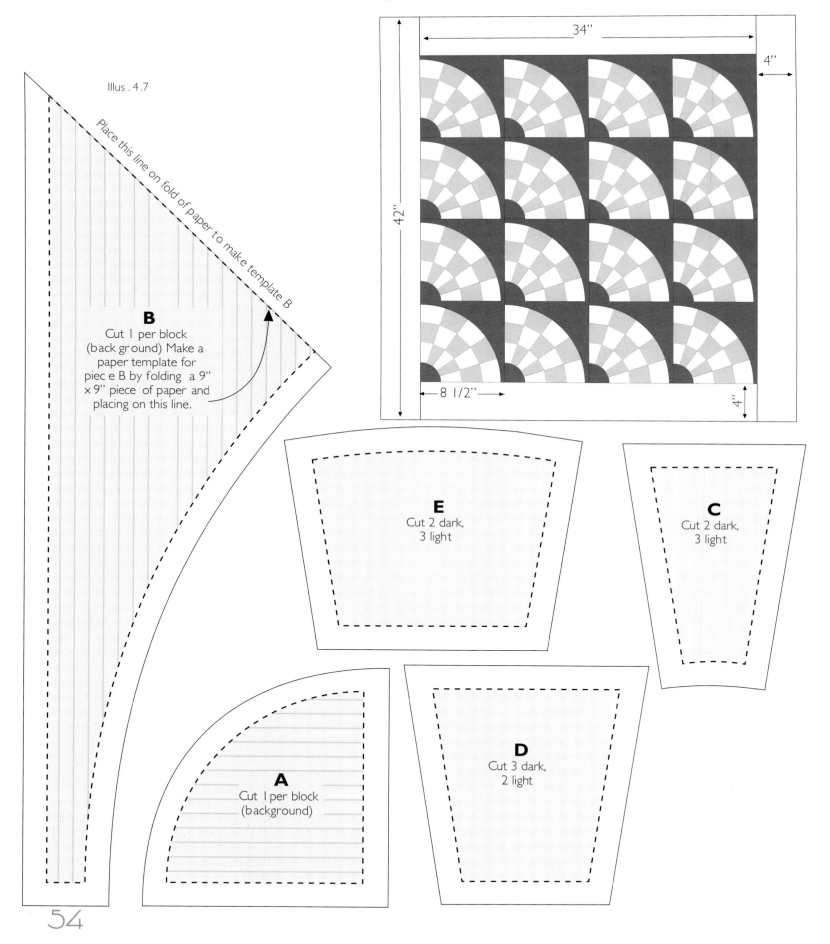

Illus . 4.7

Place this line on fold of paper to make template B

B
Cut 1 per block
(back ground) Make a
paper template for
piec e B by folding a 9"
× 9" piece of paper and
placing on this line.

34"

4"

42"

8 1/2"

4"

E
Cut 2 dark,
3 light

C
Cut 2 dark,
3 light

A
Cut 1 per block
(background)

D
Cut 3 dark,
2 light

54

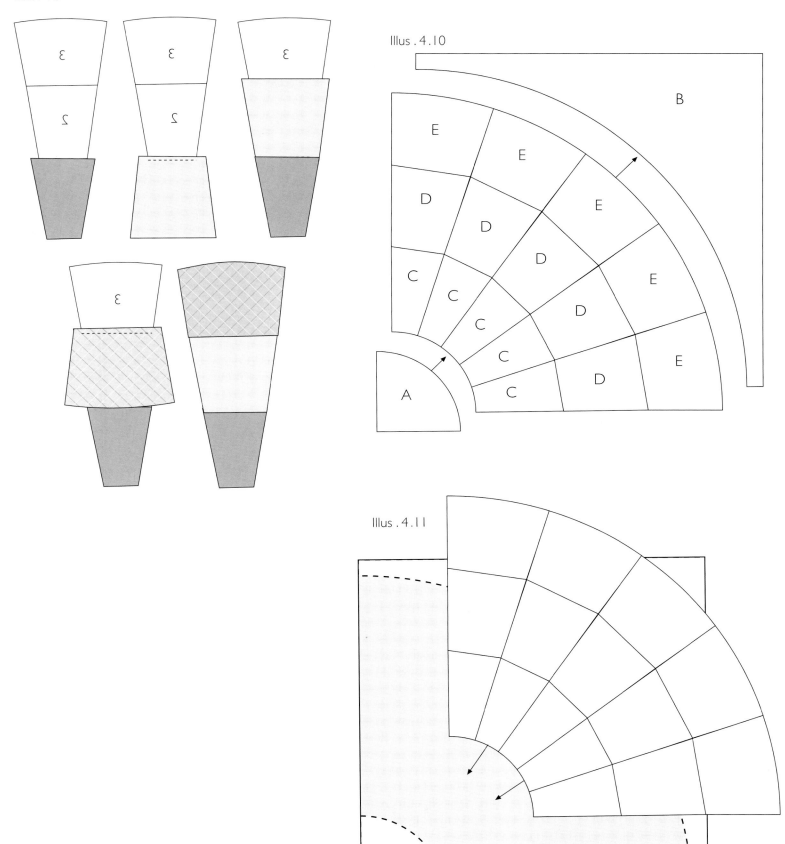

Illus . 4.9

Illus . 4.10

Illus . 4.11

9'' unfinished

55

You may photocopy this
page for your own private
use. Copy it 16 times to
paper piece a 42'' quilt.

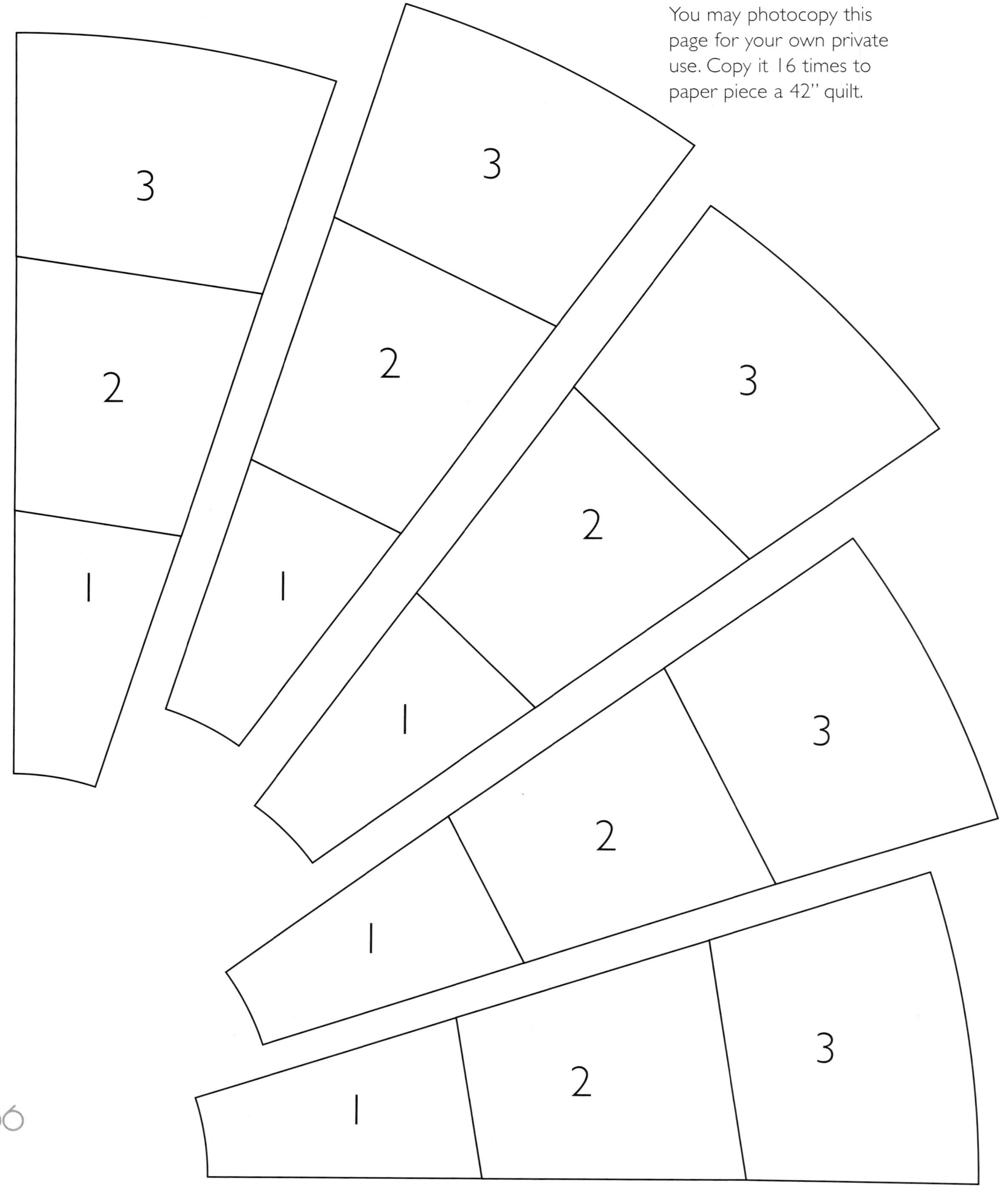

3

3

2

2

3

2

1

1

2

1

3

2

1

3

1

2

3

Illus . 4.12

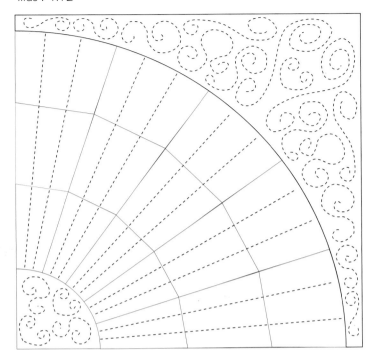

Illus . 4.13

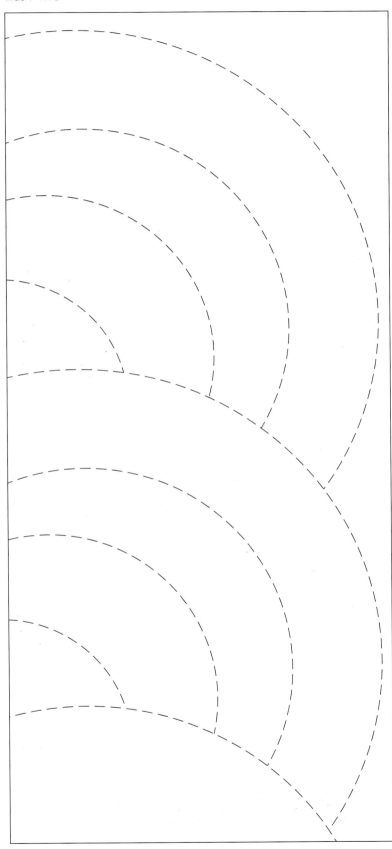

Debi Schrader's *"Work Basket and Pansy"* block reflects 1930s design in the reproduction prints, the white background and the black embroidery stitch that's both functional and decorative. Debi's new sewing machine sews a terrific copy of the old hand buttonhole embroidery. See page 164 for the full quilt. The pansy sewing tin holding various incarnations of *Work Basket* magazine and several of the other pansy collectibles are from Carol Gilham Jones's sewing room.

The Work Basket
A Little Magazine

The Kansas City company Colonial Patterns, also known by the name Aunt Martha, began selling patchwork patterns in the early 1930s. The Tillotson family, who operated the company back then, usually sold single patterns for a dime each. Occasionally, they'd offer a bargain, several patterns bundled together under the name *Aunt Martha's Work Basket*. Customers loved getting a group of patterns at a discount. In 1935, the idea evolved into a monthly magazine they named The *Work Basket*, a small publication containing patterns for all kinds of needlework - embroidery, crochet, potholders and quilts.

Aunt Martha's pattern catalogs and *Work Basket* magazine shared quilt patterns. A design first printed in the magazine might appear later in Aunt Martha's list. In 1949, the company split into two when the Tillotson family sold the Aunt Martha arm and retained the magazine in a company called Modern Handcraft, which continued to published craft and gardening magazines in the Westport area of Kansas City until the recent past.

The Work Basket & Pansy

The Work Basket magazine was cleverly designed, just the right size to fit into a sewing basket or bag. In addition to "needlecraft for pleasure and profit," readers found recipes and homey tips. "Before icing a cake place small squares of wax paper on the plate. When thoroughly dry, pull them out gently leaving the plate clean around the edge."

The "Workbasket and Pansy" block design is a simple pieced basket sprouting a pansy, similar in style to Work Basket designs published during World War II. Pansies, like Scottie dogs and polka dots, were a design rage in the mid-century years.

Rotary Cutting the Basket

Piece G: Cut a 15 7/8" square of background fabric. Cut in half diagonally to make two triangles. Save the other for another block.

Piece H: Cut a rectangle, 16 3/4" by 4 3/4", of dark pink fabric. Trim the ends at a 45-degree angle or use the template.

Piece I: Cut a rectangle, 11 1/8" by 1 7/8" of dark pink fabric. Trim the ends at a 45-degree angle or use the template.

Piece J: Cut two rectangles of background fabric, 8 7/8" by 2 1/2". Trim one end of each at a 45-degree angle or use the template.

Piece K: Cut a 7 7/8" square of background fabric. Cut it in half diagonally to make two triangles. You'll only need one. (There are no templates for G or K.)

Piecing the Basket

Pattern testers think it's best to piece the whole basket block and then do the appliqué. To do this, leave a little space unstitched between pieces G and H for the appliquéd stem. After the basket is pieced, appliqué the flower. Tuck the stem in the space and stitch the hole closed.

Illus. 5.4a

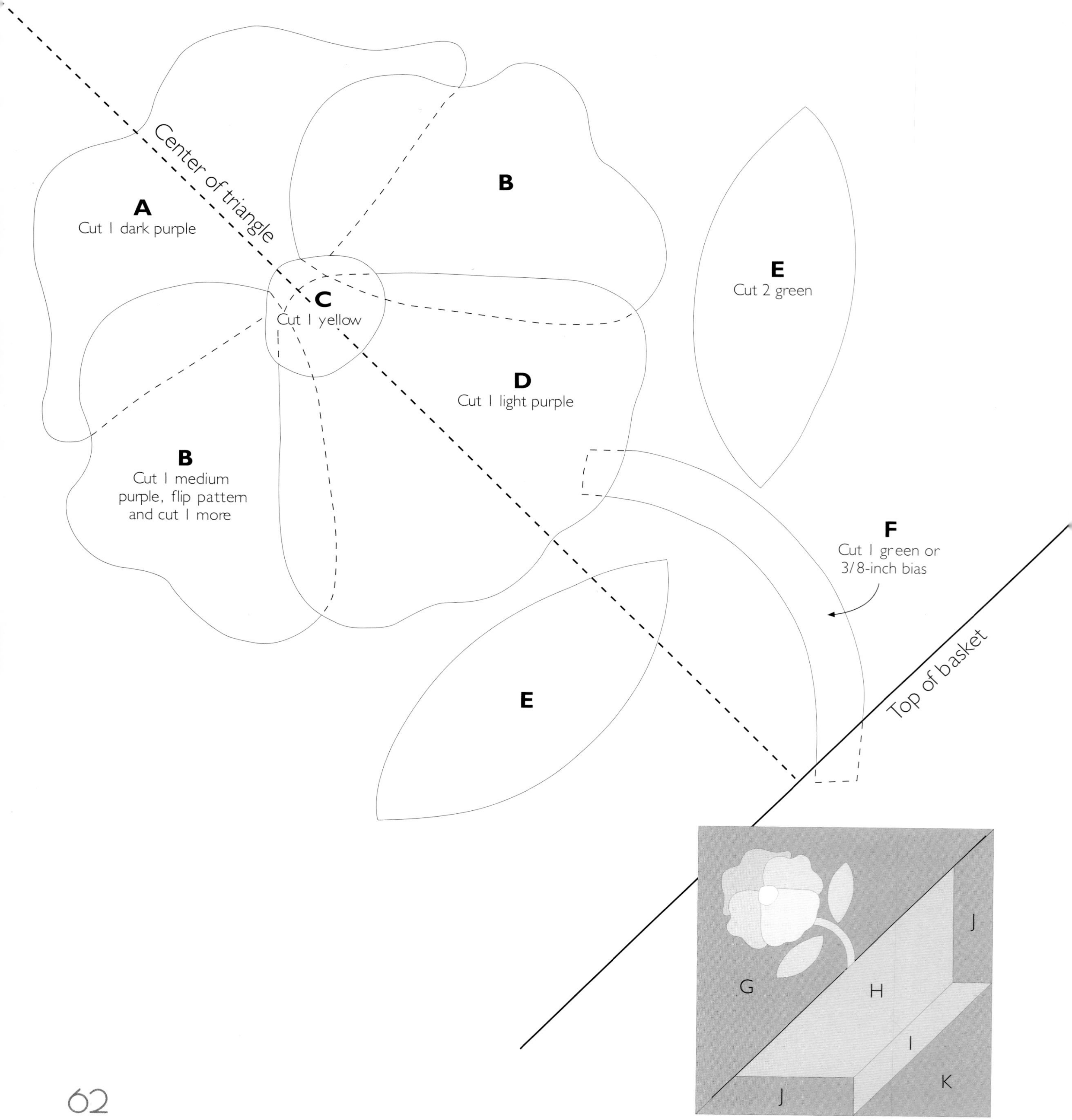
Center of triangle
A
Cut 1 dark purple
B
C
Cut 1 yellow
D
Cut 1 light purple
B
Cut 1 medium purple, flip pattern and cut 1 more
E
Cut 2 green
F
Cut 1 green or 3/8-inch bias
E
Top of basket
G
H
I
J
J
K

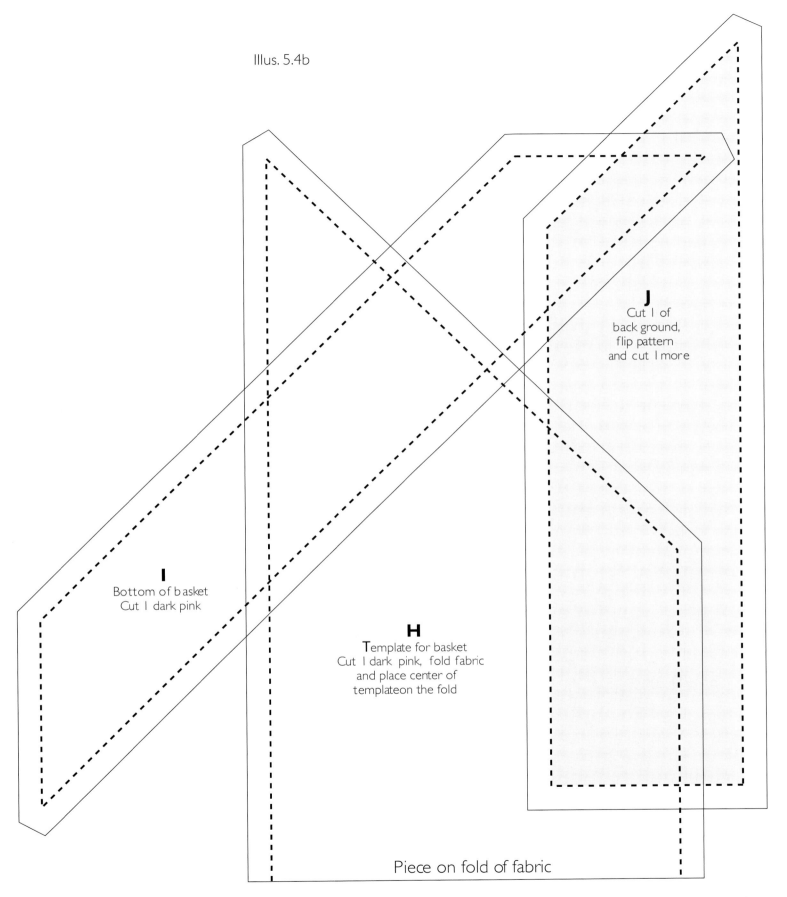

Illus. 5.4b

J
Cut 1 of
back ground,
flip pattern
and cut 1 more

I
Bottom of basket
Cut 1 dark pink

H
Template for basket
Cut 1 dark pink, fold fabric
and place center of
templateon the fold

Piece on fold of fabric

A collection of old feedsacks and patchwork potholders with new adaptations by Deb Rowden. Instructions for her dog and rooster potholders follow. Re-useable cotton sacks might contain 100 pounds of animal feed or 5 pounds of sugar as the two below the skillet did.

The original Hen and Rooster pattern from Work Basket suggested felt potholders finished with a buttonhole stitch.

The "Red-Hot Rooster" is adapted from a Work Basket design, which "your friends will exclaim [is] the cutest ever…an outstanding gift." In 1945, a pattern for a rooster panholder was given free with every subscription to Work Basket at $1 per year.

Fabric & Materials Required:

- 1 fat quarter of black fabric for the body
- 1 fat quarter of speckled fabric for the underside
- Scraps of reds, oranges and yellows for the details of beak, comb, etc.
- Two 1/2" buttons
- Thick cotton batting for padding
- Stuffing for the body

Cutting:

- Cut one 8" circle (piece C) of speckled print for the underside.
- Cut batting the same size.
- Cut two roosters (piece A) with the right sides together, adding 1/4" seam allowance to the pattern.
- Cut fabric for pieces B, D, E, F, G and H as indicated on the templates, adding a bit less than 1/4" seam allowance.
- Cut 1 layer of batting to line pieces F, G and H.

Stitching:

- Appliqué feathers (B) in place.
- Appliqué tail underfeathers (D) and tailfeathers (E), leaving ends of both feathers open so seams can be stitched later.
- Sandwich the beak (F), the comb (G) and the Wattle (H) as shown.
- Stitch, right sides together. Trim batting close to stitching and turn.
- Stitch beak, comb and wattle in place onto rooster's head, matching edges (all turned facing chicken body). Gather the comb to give it dimension.
- Stitch top of rooster together on stitching line.
- Trim excess from outer curves, clip inner curves.
- Place rooster on underside circle, right sides together. Stitch, leaving opening for turning.
- Turn with right sides out. Stitch one side of rooster to backing.
- Stuff rooster's body.
- Carefully pin, then baste stitching on other side of chicken to backing. Stitch.
- Slipstitch opening and tail feathers.
- Add button eyes.

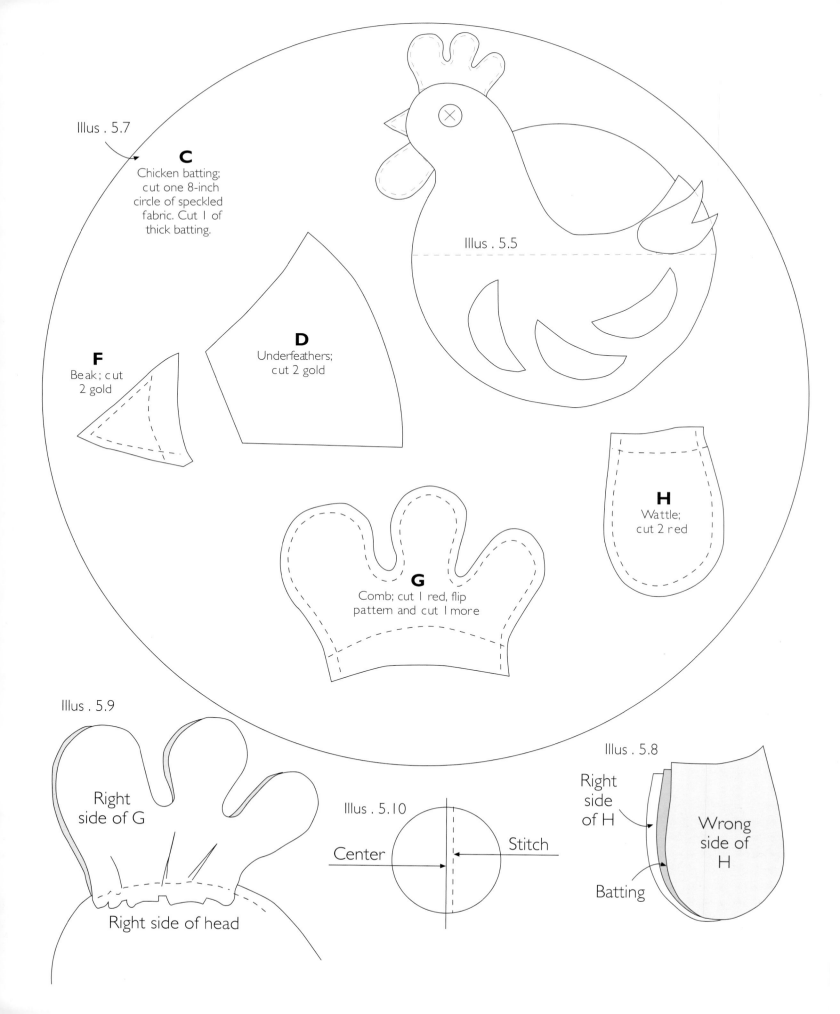

Illus . 5.7

C
Chicken batting;
cut one 8-inch
circle of speckled
fabric. Cut 1 of
thick batting.

Illus . 5.5

F
Beak; cut
2 gold

D
Underfeathers;
cut 2 gold

H
Wattle;
cut 2 red

G
Comb; cut 1 red, flip
pattern and cut 1 more

Illus . 5.9

Right
side of G

Right side of head

Illus . 5.10

Center

Stitch

Illus . 5.8

Right
side
of H

Wrong
side of
H

Batting

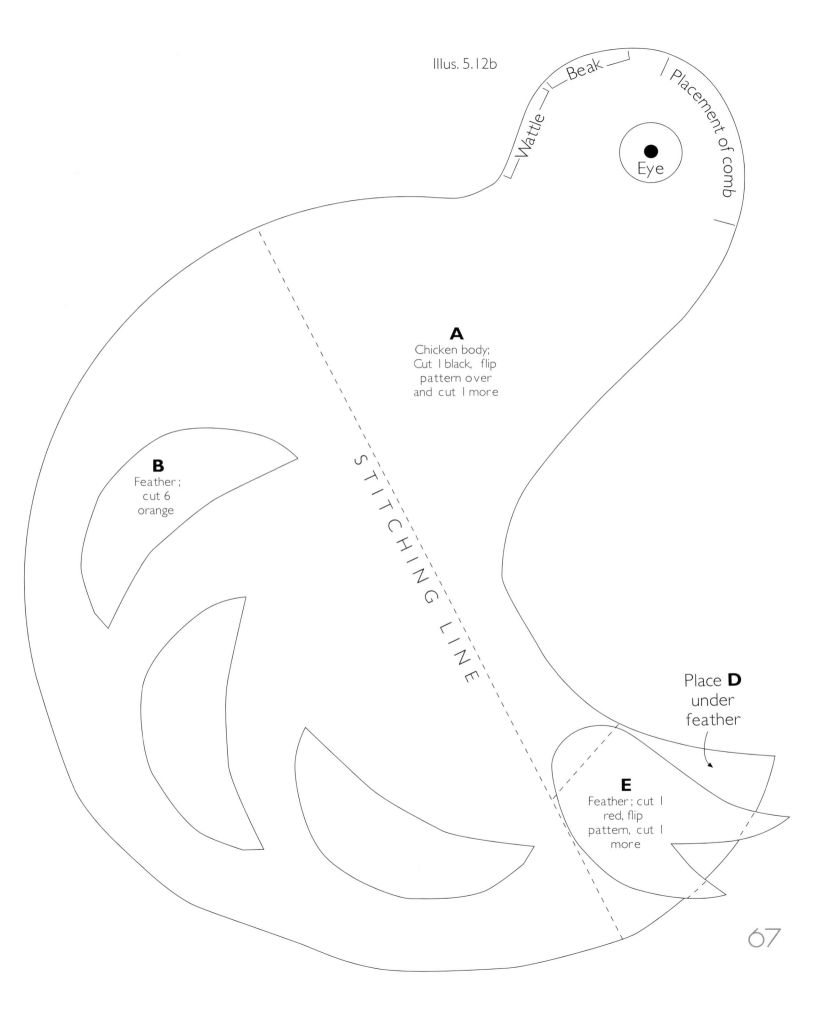

Illus. 5.12b

Wattle — Beak — Placement of comb

Eye

A
Chicken body;
Cut 1 black, flip
pattern over
and cut 1 more

B
Feather;
cut 6
orange

STITCHING LINE

Place **D**
under
feather

E
Feather; cut 1
red, flip
pattern, cut 1
more

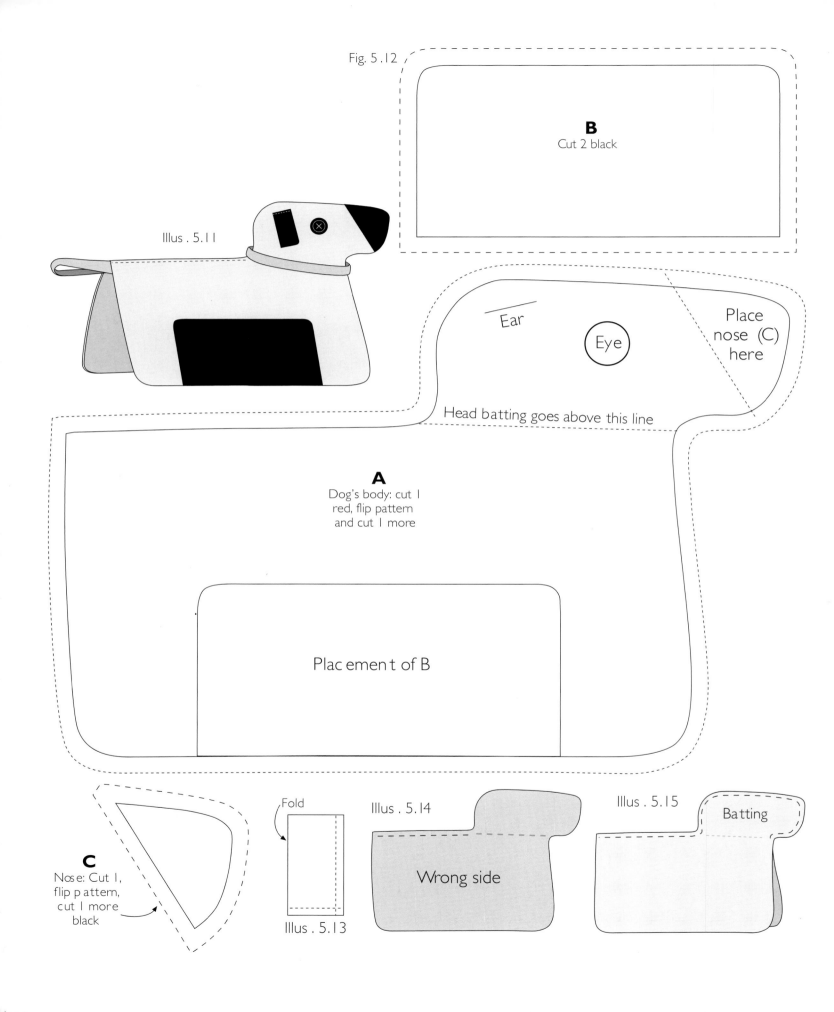

Fig. 5.12

B
Cut 2 black

Illus. 5.11

Ear

Eye

Place nose (C) here

Head batting goes above this line

A
Dog's body: cut 1 red, flip pattern and cut 1 more

Placement of B

Fold

Illus. 5.14

Wrong side

Illus. 5.15

Batting

C
Nose: Cut 1, flip pattern, cut 1 more black

Illus. 5.13

Red-Hot Dog Pot Holder

The gingham dog pot holder (see page 64) was found in an antique store. He may have been a commercial pattern, but his pedigree is unknown. The original appears to have some Scottie blood, but we turned him into a generic red mutt.

Fabric & Materials Required:

- 1 fat quarter of red for the dog
- 1 fat quarter of black for the backing and details
- Two 1/2" buttons (Deb chose rhinestones.)
- Thick cotton batting 10" x 10" for padding

Cutting:

- Cut one black backing rectangle 7" x 8".
- Using template A, cut 2 red dogs, right sides together
- Cut two black rectangles (piece B)
- Cut 2 black noses (piece C)
- For the collar and hanging tail loop, cut 1 1/4" wide bias strip of black, 12" long
- For the ears, cut 2 black squares 1 1/4".
- Cut one piece of batting 7" x 8".
- Cut 2 pieces of batting for the head (see template A)

Stitching:

- Appliqué the rectangles (B) and the noses (C) in place, leaving the outside edges raw.
- For the ears, fold the squares in half, right sides together. Stitch two edges together.
- Turn. Fold in seam on unfolded edge and press.
- Place that edge on ear stitching line.
- Stitch in place on the right side of the dog heads.
- For the collar and tail loop, stitch the long edge of the bias strip, turn inside out. Cut 4" long for the loop, 6" long for collar.
- Place dog bodies (A) right sides together.
- Stitch top of dog from neck to back, 1/4" from edge. Trim excess from outer curves, clip inner curves.
- Place the two pieces of head batting in position.
- With right sides together, stitch the batting and the head together.
- Flatten out the dog and make a sandwich of the backing square, the batting square and the flat dog. The fabric should have the wrong sides showing.
- Insert the tail loop in place so that when the dog is turned inside out the loop is on the outside. Pin.
- Stitch, leaving an opening to turn in.
- Trim batting close to stitching.
- Turn inside out and top stitch the opening together.
- Top-stitch a line along seam in middle of dog.
- Make a finished loop for the collar and pull it over the dog's head.
- Add the buttons for the eyes.

LAURA WHEELER
Collection of
Needlecraft
Masterpieces

QUILT BOOK 2

For pattern price and sending instructions, please see the publication from which you ordered this book.

When you order two or more patterns you may not receive them at the same time as they are mailed in separate wrappers.

70

Laura Wheeler
A Corporate Image

About 1933, a new quilt pattern feature began to appear in *The Kansas City Star*. In addition to Edna Marie Dunn's weekly full-sized design, drawn just for *The Star*, readers found smaller columns advertising patterns that could be ordered through the mail. A drawing of a patchwork quilt and a paragraph of description were followed by a last line reading "Send 10 cents for the pattern to *The Kansas City Star*, Needlecraft Dept., Kansas City, Mo."

Debi Schrader's version of "Laura's Calla Lily" below an antique top in the "Double Wedding Ring" design is surrounded by publications from New York's Needlecraft Service Company. A collection of tape measures, some celluloid, some enameled metal, adds to the period look. See page 164 for a view of Debi's quilt.

Laura's Calla Lily

The Star forwarded orders to a pattern source in New York City that went by a number of official names. Quilt pattern collectors know little about this company, which was formed as Needlecraft Service in 1932. The name was changed to Reader Mail in 1944. Over the years, they've offered patterns for all kinds of needlework including crochet and clothing.

Needlecraft's patterns appeared in dozens of newspapers in the 1930s. The column ran under the names Laura Wheeler or Alice Brooks, fictional authors who gave a personal touch to the feature. The Star patterns printed before World War II used no byline, so pattern collectors have learned to recognize the Needlecraft Service designs by their distinctive drawing style, which featured detailed calicoes in blocks drawn side by side to emphasize complex secondary designs. Many readers were inspired by the lovely drawings and the innovative designs to invest their dime in "stamps or coin, coin preferred."

These patterns were neither feature nor advertisement, but something called a "reader service feature." Newspapers subscribed to the feature, knowing that readers, especially rural readers, enjoyed the opportunity to order fashion and crafts by mail. The paper and the pattern company shared those many dimes.

The Needlecraft Service's New York addresses, which varied over the years, were in the neighborhood served by the Old Chelsea Station post office. Before the era of postal zones and zip codes, the words "Old Chelsea Station, New York City," were enough to direct the dime and the pattern request to the correct address.

Replies came by mail in an envelope with the return address of the local newspaper or the New York office. Pattern sheets inside were as sophisticated as the drawing in the ads, including a good deal of information on about 15 x 20 inches of tissue or newsprint.

RISING STAR IS CONVENTIONALIZED IN QUILT.

RISING STAR   PATTERN 513

Rising Star, a quilt so beautiful that anyone would consider it a prized possession, is an excellent example of the popular group of quilts that have the star for their motif. The star design of the individual block is lovely, but more lovely still is the kaleidoscopic attractive pattern produced by the joining of the blocks.
Pattern No. 513 comes to you with complete, simple, instructions for cutting, sewing and finishing, together with yardage chart, diagram of quilt to help arrange the blocks for single and double bed size, and a diagram of block which serves as a guide for placing the patches and suggests contrasting materials.
Give pattern number and allow ten days for delivery. Patterns by mail only. Send 10 cents for the quilt pattern to The Kansas City Star, Needlecraft Dept., Kansas City, Mo.

"Rising Star" is a typical early '30s pattern from the Needlecraft Service Company, highlighting original design with sophisticated secondary patterning. In some newspapers the feature appeared under the signature Laura Wheeler, but the early *Star* patterns were anonymous.

Quilt historian Wilene Smith has determined that Nathan Kogan, Max Levine and Anne Borne formed a business called Needlecraft Service, Inc. in 1932. As yet, pattern historians know nothing about the actual designers who created the innovative patterns and drawings. To add to confusion about company history, Smith found that Needlecraft Service set up two competing branches to make the most of cities with competing newspapers. Laura Wheeler might offer patterns in one paper, Alice Brooks in another. Each "designer" had a different New York City address, which Smith thinks were mail drops, to distinguish the bylines. The company also used regional names such as Carol Curtis in the Midwest and Mary Cullen in the northwest. Marian Martin and Anne Adams were additional bylines, primarily for clothing patterns.

"Laura's Calla Lily" is named for the Needlecraft Service's fictional columnist. Typical of the Needlecraft style is a striped basket, a rather modern look. The flower, originally named "Garden Treasure" was adapted from the popular "Double Wedding Ring" design of the time, a national fad.

Rotary Cutting the Basket

Piece J: Cut one 15 7/8" square of background fabric. Cut in half diagonally to make two triangles. You'll need one.

Piece K: Cut one rectangle, 13 5/8" by 1 5/8", of light green fabric. Trim the ends at a 45-degree angle or use the template.

Piece L: Cut a rectangle, 11 1/2" by 2", of dark green fabric. Trim the ends at a 45-degree angle or use the template.

Piece M: Cut a rectangle, 8 1/2" by 2", of light green fabric. Trim one end of each at a 45-degree angle or use the template.

Piece N: Cut a rectangle, 10" by 2 3/4", of dark green fabric. Trim the ends of each at a 45-degree angle or use the template.

Piece O: Cut a 7" square of background. Cut in half diagonally to make two triangles. You'll need one.

Piece P: Cut two rectangles, 9 5/8" by 3 5/8", of background fabric. Trim the end of each at a 45 degree angle or use the template. (There are no templates for J or O.)

Piecing the Basket

Pattern testers think it's best to piece the whole basket block and then do the appliqué. To do this, leave a little space unstitched between pieces J and K for the appliquéd stem. After the basket is pieced, appliqué the flower. Tuck the leaves in the space and stitch the hole closed.

Stitching the Calla Lily

You can piece the lily in conventional fashion, but if you are skillful at the modern technique of paper piecing (machine stitching over the paper pattern), try that. To conventionally piece, cut pieces A, G, H and I as indicated, adding 1/4 inch seams and piece as shown.

Prepare the edges of the flower for appliqué. Place piece B as shown and top with the flower.

Fashion the two toned leaves by cutting a large leaf and then appliquéing a half leaf on top. Place the prepared leaves over the flower and under the basket as shown.

Illus. 6.6a

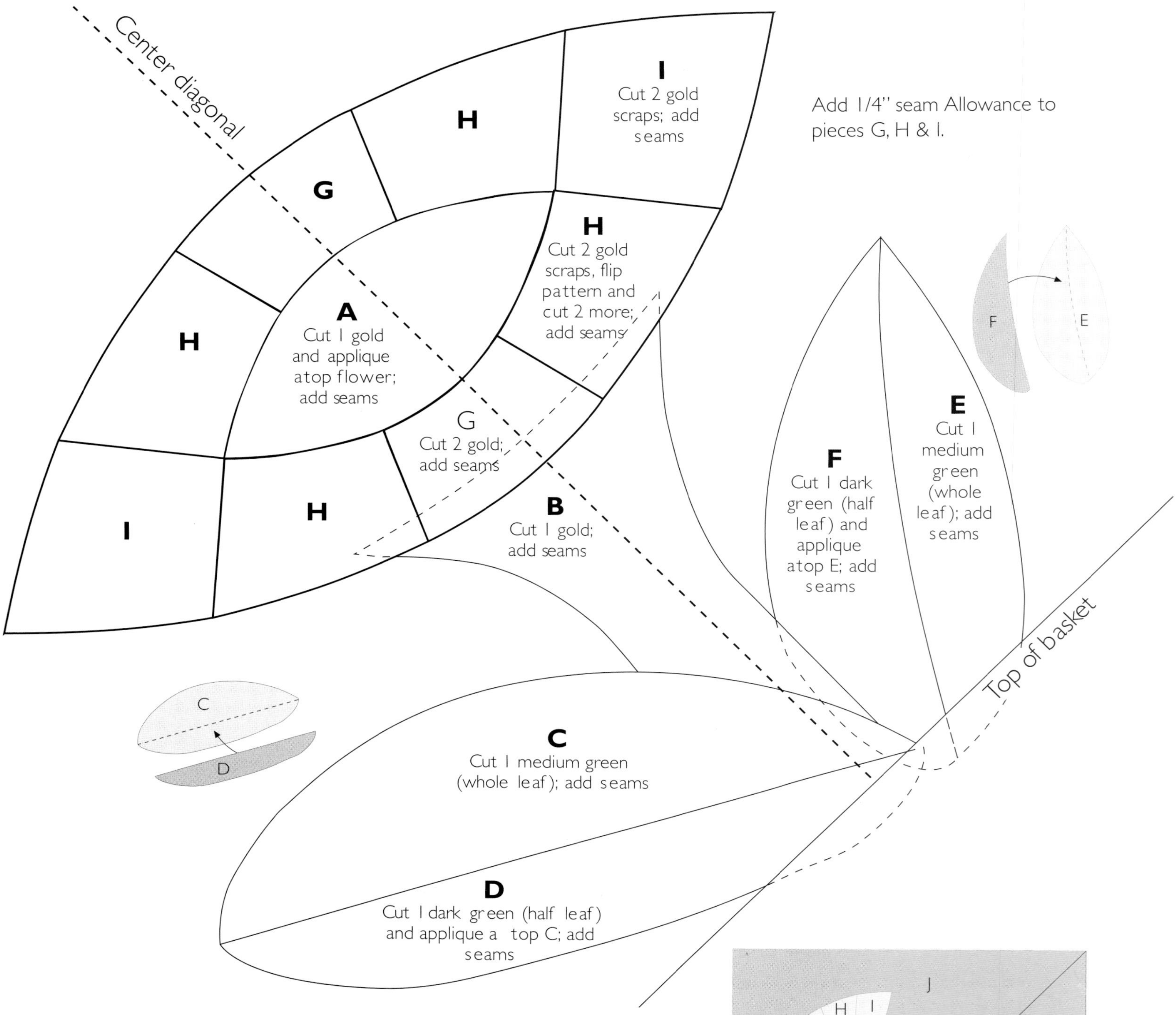

Center diagonal

I
Cut 2 gold scraps; add seams

H

G

Add 1/4" seam Allowance to pieces G, H & I.

H
Cut 2 gold scraps, flip pattern and cut 2 more; add seams

H

A
Cut 1 gold and applique atop flower; add seams

G
Cut 2 gold; add seams

H

I

B
Cut 1 gold; add seams

F   E

E
Cut 1 medium green (whole leaf); add seams

F
Cut 1 dark green (half leaf) and applique atop E; add seams

Top of basket

C

D

C
Cut 1 medium green (whole leaf); add seams

D
Cut 1 dark green (half leaf) and applique a top C; add seams

Piecing the flower

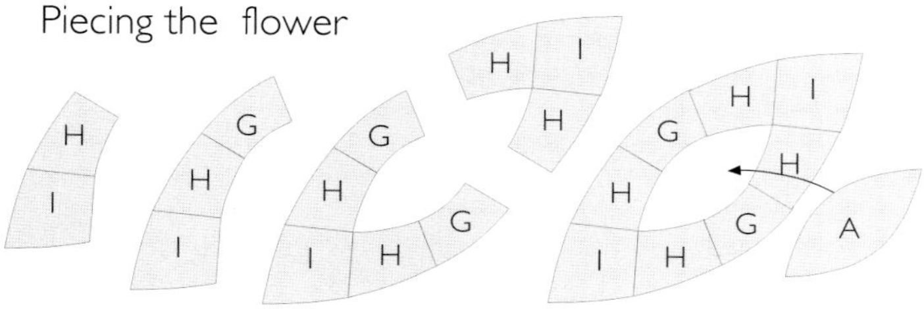

H I   H G I   H G I   H G I   H
I   H   H   H   A
       I   I H   I H G
                         G

J
H I
G H
A
H G H
I H B F E
C K   P
D L
M
N
P   O

76

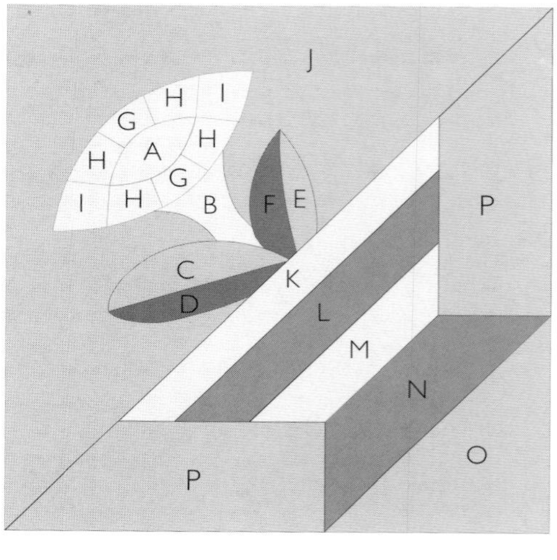

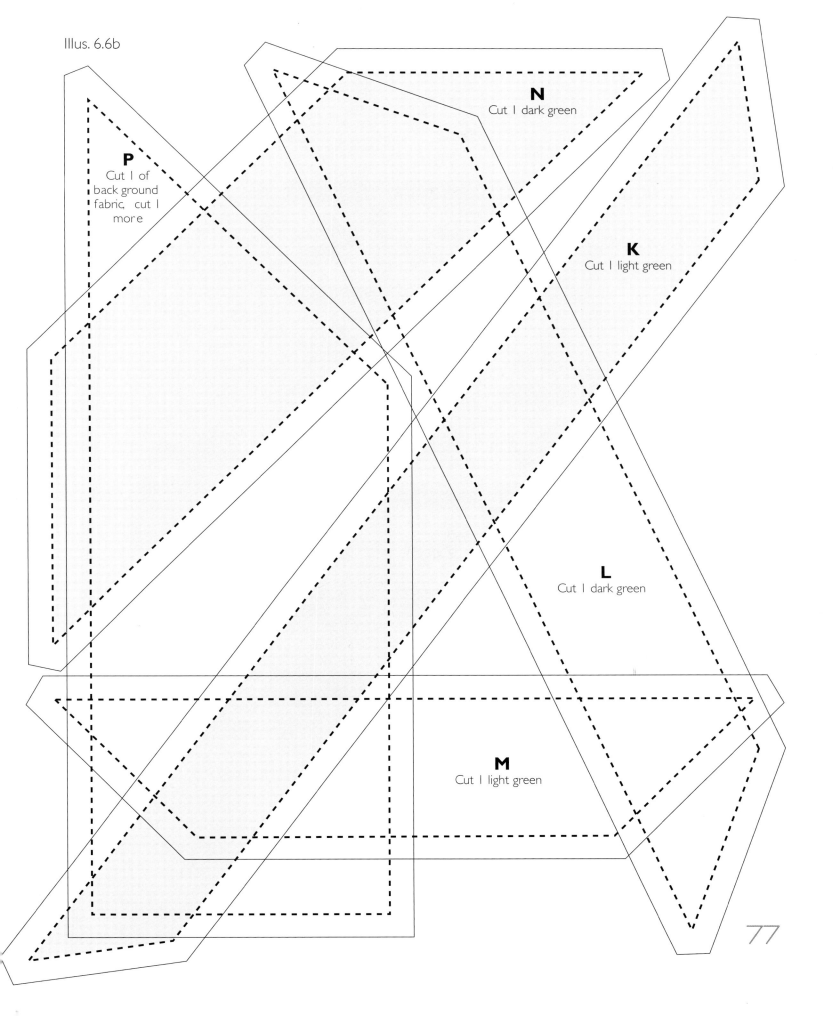

Illus. 6.6b

N
Cut 1 dark green

P
Cut 1 of
back ground
fabric, cut 1
more

K
Cut 1 light green

L
Cut 1 dark green

M
Cut 1 light green

77

Pups & Plaids

Pups and Plaids by Barbara Brackman, Lawrence, Kansas. Hand appliquéd and hand quilted. 32'' x 42''.

In mid-century needlework columns, Scotties decorated dishtowels, potholders, quilts and kids' clothing. Few quilt designers resisted the temptation to draw a Scottie design, some with more success than others. The well-loved and well-used quilt on the table top was made by Thelma Tunison Poore in Kansas City in the 1940s, and is in the collection of her granddaughter Deb Rowden.

Pups & Plaids Quilt

32" x 42"

8" Block

Scottish Terriers were a beloved image in the 1930s and '40s. The breed was introduced to the world in the 19th century by Queen Victoria who loved both dogs and things Scottish. Collies and Scotties owe much of their popularity to the Queen's kennel. President Franklin D. Roosevelt also owned a Scottie, as does President George W. Bush. Roosevelt's Scottie, Fala, was so much a part of his public image that the FDR Memorial in Washington D.C. includes a sculptured portrait of the dog.

In contrast to their rather sophisticated pieced designs, appliqué patterns from Laura Wheeler tended to be simple. Nursery animals were a specialty. The feature offered a pattern in *The Star* similar to this particular Scottie, which was drawn from a 1950's felt sweater appliqué.

You'll need:

- 12 Blocks finishing to 8"
- 2" Sashing & Border

Scottie dogs and plaids are an enduring combination. All the fabrics in this quilt are plaids, either woven or printed. The woven plaids, dyed in the yarn stage and woven into pattern, are a bit of a challenge for beginners because they tend to stretch more than prints. This quilt is so simple, however, that you should have no trouble keeping it square if you pre-wash your fabrics so the weave shrinks and becomes a little tighter. Be sure to check the black and red plaids for bleeding by placing a small piece of a yellow plaid in their wash water. If a dark bleeds onto the yellow, don't use the dark.

Yellow Plaids:
- For the backgrounds buy at least 4 different quarter yard pieces (fat quarters or long quarters)

Black Plaids
- For the Scotties buy at least 4 different black plaids in quarter yard pieces for variety, and an extra 3/4 of a yard of one of them for the sashing.

Red Plaids
Buy at least 4 different red plaids in quarter yard pieces for the bows and setting squares plus an extra quarter yard (long, measuring 9" x 44") of one of them for the binding.

Backing

- 1 1/4 yards

Cutting

The Blocks

- Cut 12 squares 8-1/2" for appliqué backgrounds
- Cut Scottie dogs and bows as indicated on the pattern templates adding a bit less than 1/4" for seam allowance.

The Sashing & Border

- Cut 20 squares 2-1/2" from the various red plaids for the cornerstones
- Cut 31 rectangles 2-1/2" by 8-1/2" from the black plaid.

Stitching the Blocks

■ For information about books that teach hand and machine appliqué see page 8.

■ Prepare the appliqué pieces using your favorite method.

■ Press the backgrounds to create horizontal and vertical creases for placement.

■ Glue, baste or pin the Scotties in place using the guidelines on the pattern.

■ Then place the bows.

■ Stitch the pieces down using your favorite technique.

Setting the Quilt

■ Press the blocks and trim the edges to make unfinished blocks 8" square

■ Add black sashing rectangles between the blocks as shown below making 4 strips of 3 blocks each.

■ Stitch together alternating red squares and black rectangles to make the horizontal sashing as shown below. Make 5 strips of 4 red squares and 3 black rectangles.

■ Set the blocks between the strips.

■ Press quilt top and trim edges if necessary.

Illus . 6.12

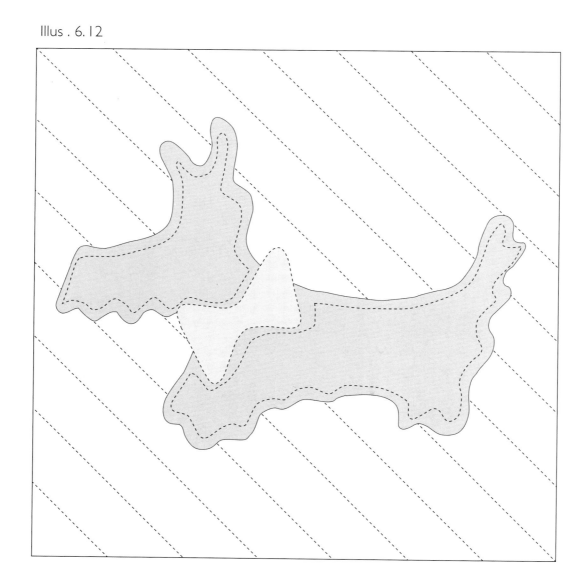

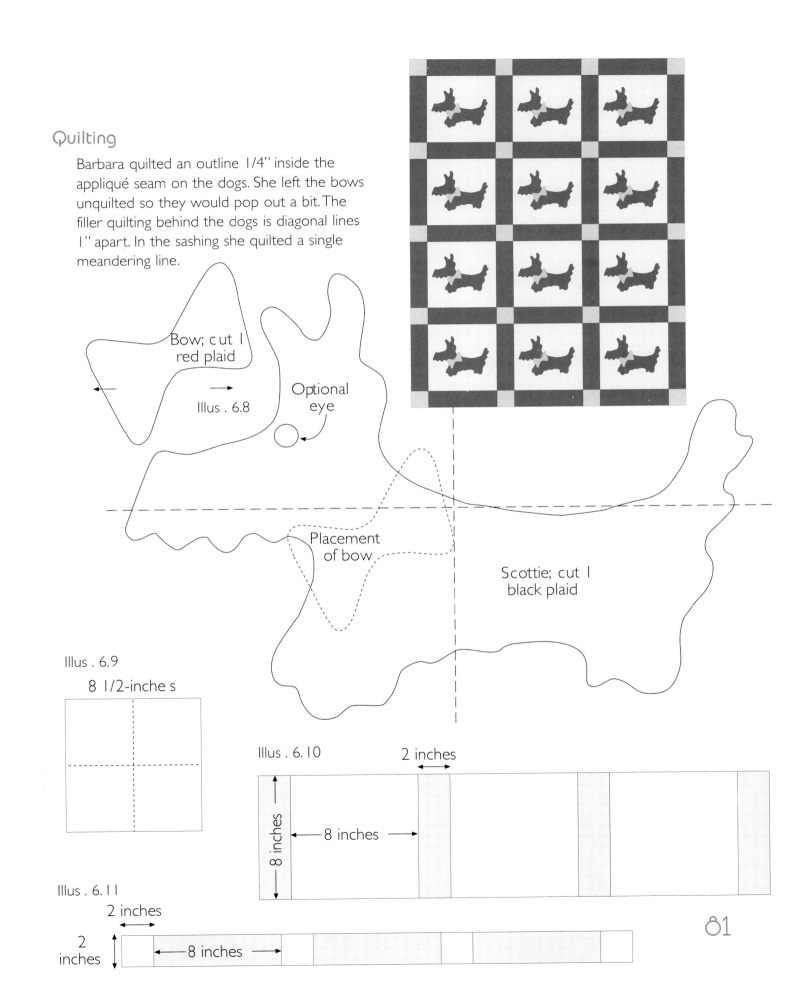

Quilting

Barbara quilted an outline 1/4" inside the appliqué seam on the dogs. She left the bows unquilted so they would pop out a bit. The filler quilting behind the dogs is diagonal lines 1" apart. In the sashing she quilted a single meandering line.

Bow; cut 1
red plaid

Illus . 6.8

Optional
eye

Placement
of bow

Scottie; cut 1
black plaid

Illus . 6.9

8 1/2-inches

Illus . 6.10

2 inches

8 inches

8 inches

Illus . 6.11

2 inches

2
inches

8 inches

Deb Lybarger stitched her sampler from a variety of fabrics that her husband brought home from Japan, including a latticework print that makes an excellent basket.

For a view of her quilt top see page 12. Below is a block from the 1930s, a version of Hubert Ver Mehren's original tulip, showing the combination of appliqué and embroidery typical of his stamped patterns. Asiatic design fascinated Americans. The sewing basket embellished with glass beads and Chinese coins contains clippings from *The Star* and one of Ver Mehren's pattern booklets that could be ordered for a quarter.

Hubert Ver Mehren
A Man in a Woman's World

Editors at *The Kansas City Star* knew how Depression era readers loved the quilt pattern features, so they subscribed to two different mail-order patterns. Quilters looked forward to the full-sized Sunday pattern drawn by Edna Marie Dunn. During the week, they read two smaller reader service features, one from New York's Needlecraft Service, the other from a Des Moines company known to pattern collectors as Home Art Studios.

Like the Laura Wheeler feature, Home Art Studios sent The Star a weekly advertisement featuring a drawing of a quilt with information about the design and instructions to send a dime or a quarter to "Pattern Department," in care of *The Star*. *The Star* forwarded the orders to Des Moines. Again, the columns were anonymous in Kansas City, although some newspapers used the byline "Bettina."

Debi Schrader of Kansas City, Kansas teaches classes in modifying factory-made clothing to create unique jackets. Here she's cut a black crew-neck sweatshirt, appliquéd "Hubert's Royal Tulips" to the trimmed bottom and bound the raw edges with a plaid cotton cut on the bias. A purchased "frog" fastening in Chinese style completes the look.

The old calendar marks September 22, 1928, the inauguration of *The Kansas City Star's* pattern series. On the table, Bakelite jewelry is arranged with antique handerkerchiefs. An ambitious seamstress with a very fine hand appliquéd Gertrude's name in tiny bias strips.

"Star of France" from Ver Mehren's catalog *Colonial Quilts* has nothing old fashioned about it. Quilters could buy a kit or a stamped pattern for this challenging design.

Bettina was the pen name of a man. Hubert Ver Mehren (1892-1972) had inherited a mail-order notions company from his father, a company that had two branches, the ideal Button and Pleating Company, in Omaha, Nebraska, where Hubert grew up, and the Iowa Button and Pleating Company in Des Moines, the branch Hubert managed after his World War I service and 1920 marriage. They sold notions such as braid and beads through mail-order catalogs and did pleating, scalloping, buttonholes and hem-stitching to order. The companies also stamped cloth with patterns for needlework-corset covers, collars, tablecloths and pillow cases.

As colorfast cotton embroidery floss in a variety of shades became widely available, Hubert realized there was a market for stamped quilt blocks to be embroidered. He also realized he could stamp fabric for geometric patchwork, making kits for pieced designs. With his wife Mary Jacobs, he ran a thriving quilt pattern business between 1931 and 1934.

Hubert's Royal Tulips

Uer Mehren was quite a draftsman. His stamped kits for complex stars and sunbursts that covered the whole quilt top became a trademark. The medallions offered a real challenge to skilled seamstresses, who must have been pleased with his accuracy. The bread and butter of Home Art's business, however, was the stamped blocks, pillow cases and dresser scarves that appealed to the average seamstress. Although the company's heyday was short (Mary became ill and Hubert devoted time to caring for her and then raising their children after her death), Home Art Studios strongly influenced the look of mid-twentieth century quilts.

The inspiration for "Hubert's Royal Tulips" was his stamped design reflecting art nouveau ideas. The original called for a combination of embroidery and appliqué, a look that was more popular in the 1930s than it is today. The basket, one he called the "Royal Japanese Vase," seems to owe little to any Asian art traditions, but is, instead, a classic patchwork basket.

Rotary Cutting the Basket

Piece I: Cut one 15 7/8" square of background fabric. Cut in half diagonally to make two triangles. You will need one.

Piece J: Cut a 9 5/8" square of light blue fabric. Cut in half diagonally to make two triangles. You'll need one.

Piece K: Cut a 4" square of light blue. Cut each in half diagonally to make two triangles.

Piece L: Cut a rectangle, 9 5/8" by 3 5/8", of background fabric. Trim the ends at a 45-degree angle or use the template.

Piece M: Cut a 7" square of background fabric. Cut it in half diagonally to make two triangles. You'll only need one. (There are no templates for I, J, K, or M.)

Piecing the Basket

Appliqué handle pieces G, before piecing the block. Piece the whole basket block and then do the rest of the appliqué. To do this, leave a little space unstitched between piece J and the bottom half of the basket for the appliquéd stem. After the basket is pieced, appliqué the flower. Tuck the stem in the space and stitch the hole closed.

Illus. 7.4a

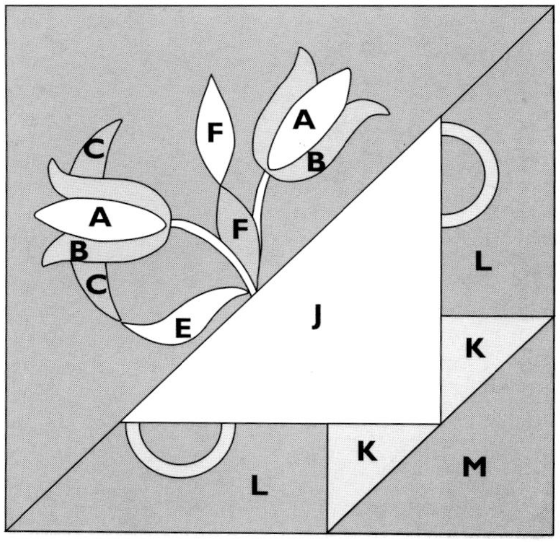
F
A
C
B
A
F
B
C
E
J
L
K
K
L
M

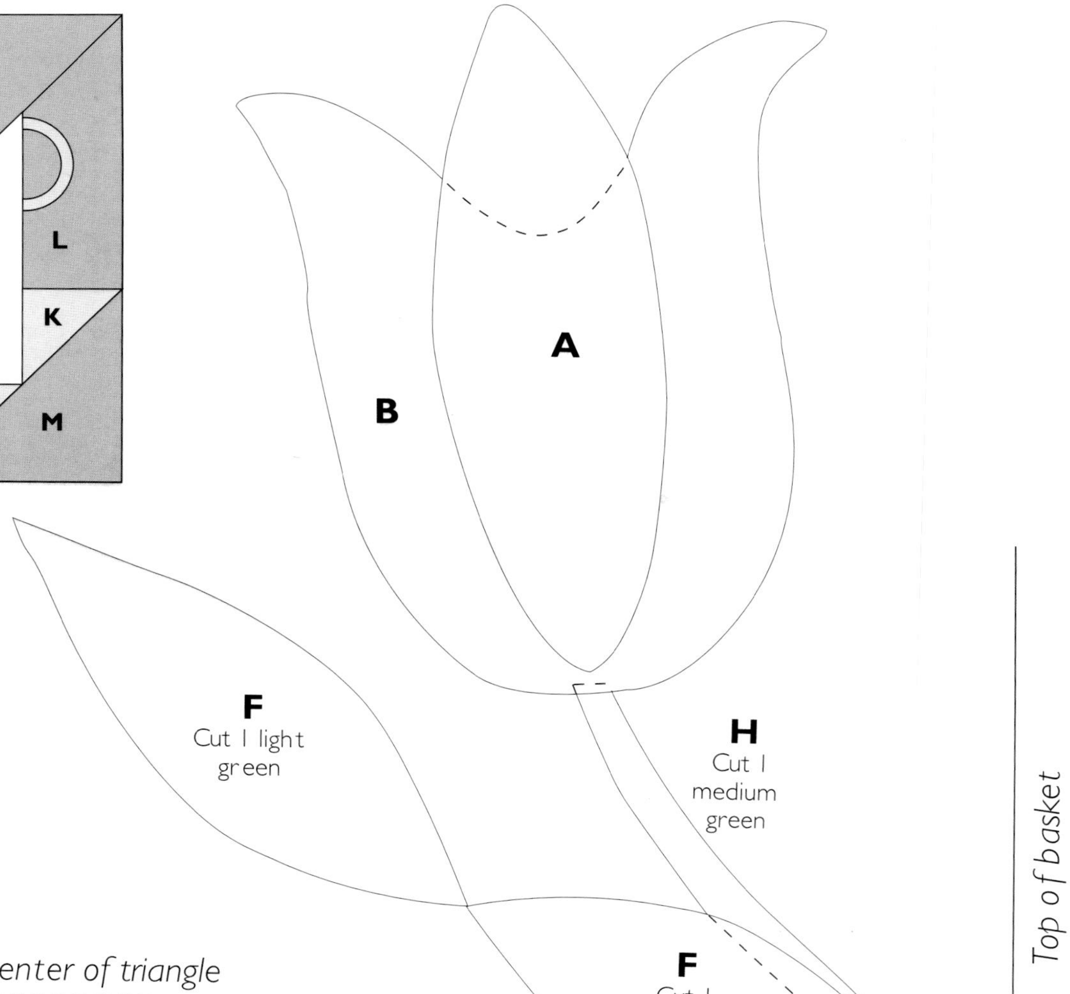
A
B
F
Cut 1 light green
H
Cut 1 medium green
Top of basket
Center of triangle

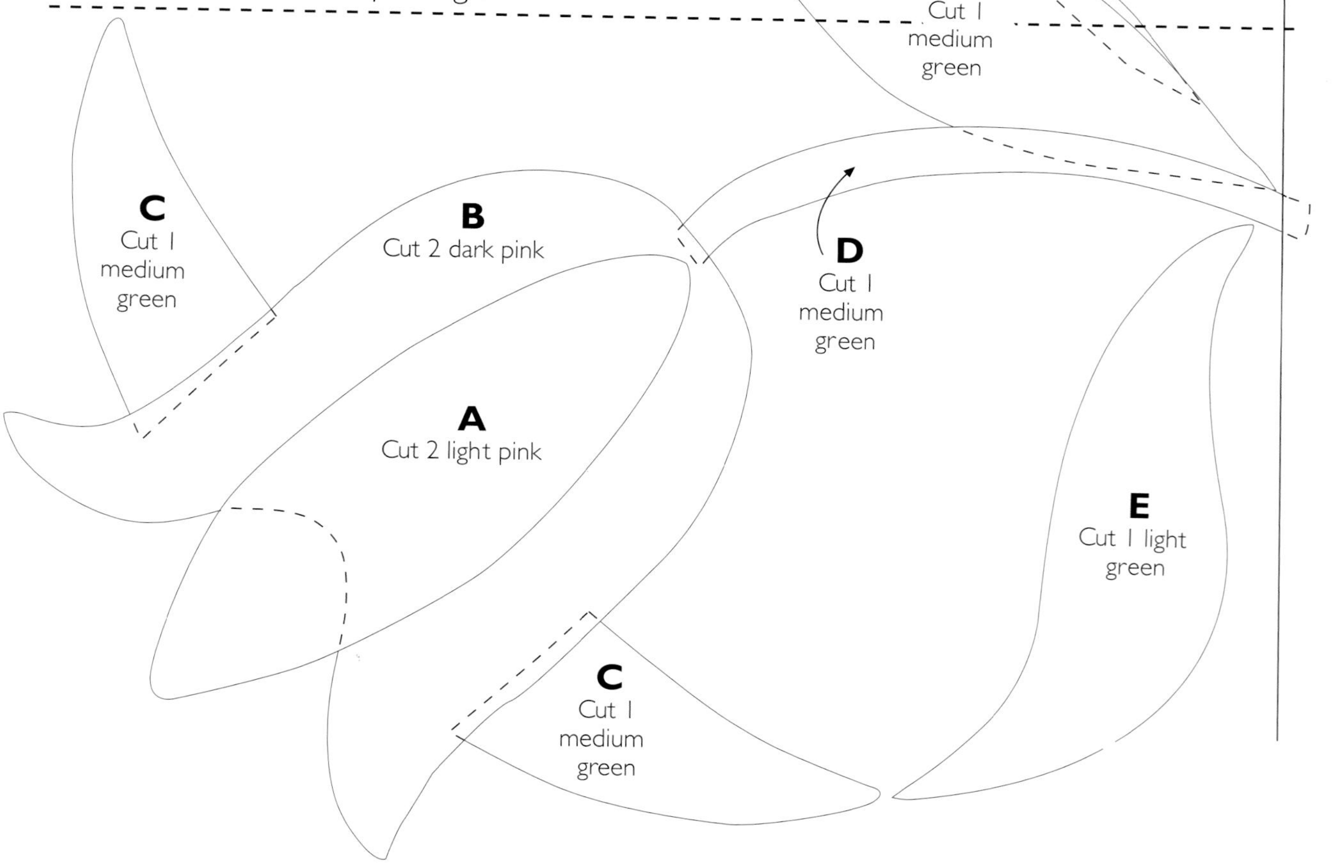
F
Cut 1 medium green
C
Cut 1 medium green
B
Cut 2 dark pink
D
Cut 1 medium green
A
Cut 2 light pink
E
Cut 1 light green
C
Cut 1 medium green

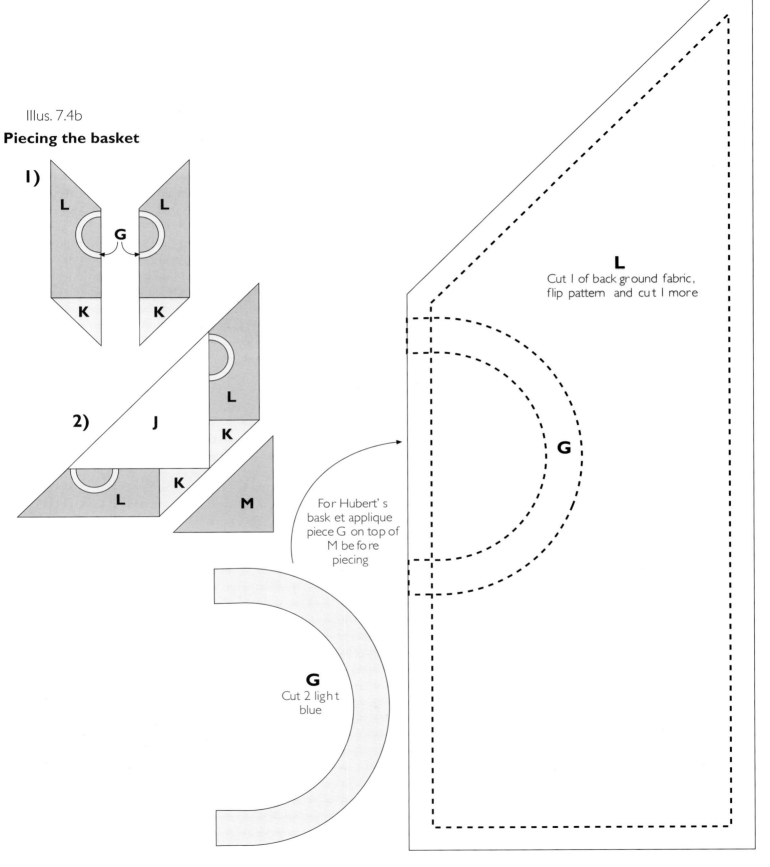

Illus. 7.4b
Piecing the basket

1)

L L
G
K K

2)
J
L
K
K
L
M

For Hubert's basket applique piece G on top of M before piecing

L
Cut 1 of background fabric, flip pattern and cut 1 more

G

G
Cut 2 light blue

89

"Carlie's Wild Rose" by Jean Pearson Stanclift with several reproduction booklets and an original quilt article by Carlie Sexton. The ad for Quaint Quilts includes an order form for her first pamphlet, published in 1922. For another view of Jean's *Where The Wild Flowers Grow,* see the cover.

Carlie Sexton
Free-Lance Historian

Like Kansas City, Des Moines was an important town for needlework design. Hubert Ver Mehren, the Wallace Publishing Company, the Meredith Corporation (still publishing *Better Homes & Gardens*), and Carlie Sexton mailed out many a quilt pattern postmarked from the Iowa capitol.

Carlie Sexton (1877-1964) wrote about quilts for several periodicals in the teens, twenties and thirties. Her articles were popular enough to encourage her to start a pattern business that she operated from her home, a classic quilt cottage industry. Sexton's patterns tended towards the traditional, although she occasionally designed one of her own with a modern look.

Carlie Sexton was born November 4, 1877 in Pella, Iowa, daughter of Francis Marion Sexton and Emma Jane Rea Sexton. Carlie was apparently her given name, an aunt's nickname. Her family suffered from tuberculosis, which killed her mother when Carlie was five years old and her father when she was 26. Carlie was raised by her mother's sister, the aunt she was named for, Mary Caroline Raney.

Quilt Historian Susan Price Miller has traced Sexton's magazine work to *People's Popular Monthly,* a Des Moines magazine that began in the late nineteenth century. She began working there as a clerk in 1907, when she was thirty. Ten years later she was in charge of the circulation department. She probably wrote unsigned articles about quilts for the magazine beginning in the teens.

Carlie's Wild Rose

In April, 1920, a byline appeared on a quilt article, suggesting that readers write Sexton for the patterns. By 1922, she had quit the magazine and was running a pattern business with some help from her stepmother and sister.

Throughout the 1920s and '30s, she continued to write free-lance articles for magazines such as *Successful Farming* and *Holland's Magazine*. Her pattern catalogs and her magazine articles featured designs drawn from antique quilts. At first, she copied designs from family quilts, then conducted contests to obtain designs from antiques and traveled around the Midwest looking for inspiration.

Rotary Cutting the Basket

Piece J: Cut one 15 7/8" square of background fabric. Cut in half diagonally to make two triangles. You will need one.

Piece K: Cut a 9 5/8" square of striped fabric, being careful that the stripes follow the block's diagonal axis. Cut in half diagonally to make two triangles. You'll need one.

Piece L: Cut a 4" square of striped fabric, being careful that the stripes run diagonally across the square. Cut each in half diagonally to make two triangles.

Piece M: Cut a rectangle, 9 5/8" by 3 5/8"es, of background fabric. Trim the ends at a 45-degree angle or use the template.

Piece N: Cut a 7" square of background fabric. Cut it in half diagonally to make two triangles. You'll only need one. (There are no templates for J, K, L, or N.)

Piecing the Basket

Appliqué the handle piece to the background before piecing the block. Then piece the whole basket. After the basket is pieced, appliqué the flower with the leaves covering the stem.

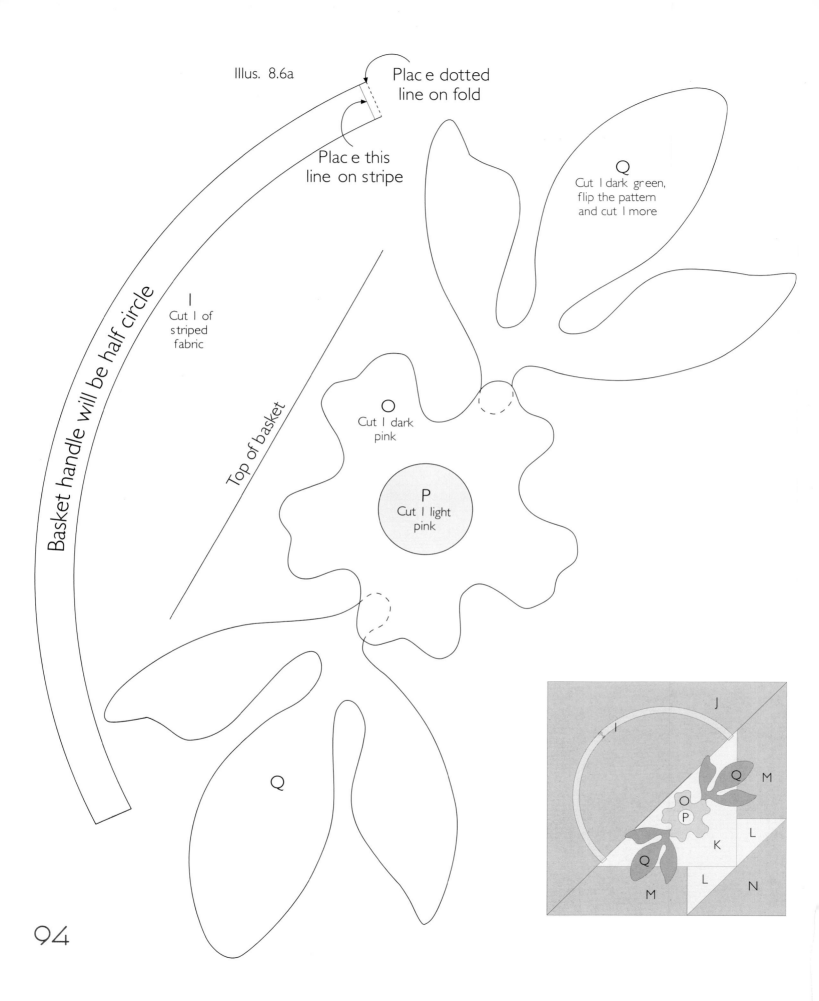

Illus. 8.6a

Place dotted line on fold

Place this line on stripe

Basket handle will be half circle

I
Cut 1 of striped fabric

Top of basket

Q
Cut 1 dark green, flip the pattern and cut 1 more

O
Cut 1 dark pink

P
Cut 1 light pink

Q

Sexton wrote in one of her catalogs, "I find a great number of wonderfully pretty old quilts in my jaunts into the country, village or city." Quilt historian Barbara Bannister, who corresponded with her in the early 1960s, wrote that Sexton "was very interested in old appliqué quilts. She wrote about how she sometimes would see some real 'finds' on a clothesline and would stop in to talk to owner, etc. and then draft a pattern."

Sexton lived with the Raneys until she married in 1927. At the age of 47, she married Harold A. Holmes, a man she had worked with at *People's Popular Monthly* in the teens. The circumstances of their courtship invite some romantic speculation because their marriage took place two weeks after the death of Holmes's first wife. Holmes had been living in Chicago since 1920. The couple soon built a house in Wheaton, Illinois, a Chicago suburb, with a studio, the "Hobby House" for the quilt pattern business. Harold, who was in the advertising and graphic arts business, died in 1944. Carlie died in Wheaton at 87, twenty years later.

"Carlie's Wild Rose" combines two of her original patterns, the "Wild Rose," with the "Flower Basket." Her genius was in cutting a simple basket from striped fabric and appliquéing a floral on the basket rather than in it. For another version of this basket see page 98.

A photograph of quilts on the line from Sexton's pamphlet *Old-Fashioned Quilts* gives a glimpse of the antiques that were her inspiration.

This piece is for the 15''
version of Carlie's Wild Rose

Illus. 8.6b

Piecing the basket

1)

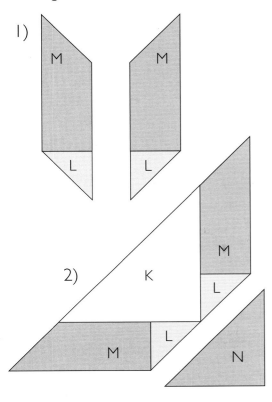

2)

M
Cut 1 of back ground fabric ,
flip pattern and cut 1 more

Carlie's Wild Rose by Jean Pearson Stanclift and Barbara Brackman, Lawrence, Kansas. Machine quilted by Jeanne Zyck. 51-1/2" x 51-1/2". A collection of mid-century art pottery on a painted oak bureau picks up the blue-green of the appliquéd leaves.

Carlie's Wild Rose

51 1/2 Square Quilt 10 Blocks

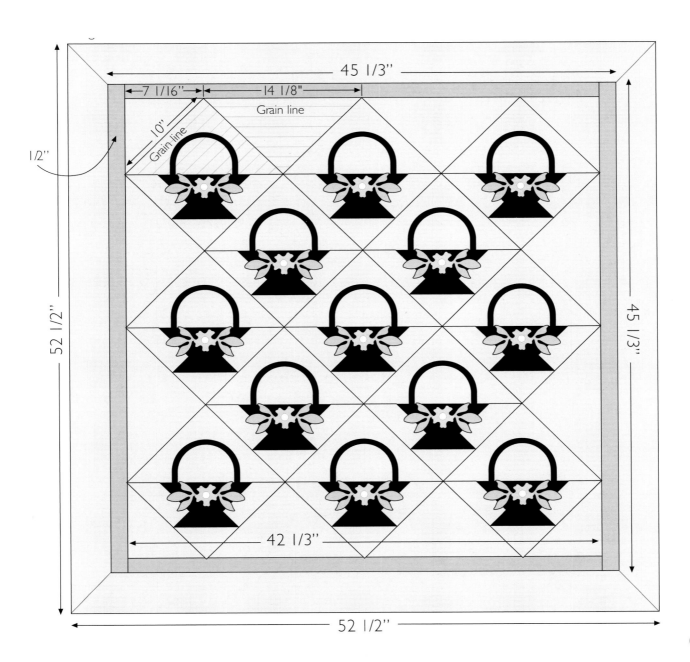

Fig. 8.9

Fig. 8.10

Fig. 8.11

Fig. 8.12

Carlie's Wild Rose

51 1/2" Square Quilt
10" Blocks

Choose your favorite of the 13 baskets in *The Star Magazine* this year and repeat the block for a wall quilt by redrafting the pattern to a smaller size. Carlie Sexton's basket of striped fabric looks up-to-date in black and white with red and teal green accents. Below, we give you a pattern for a 10" block.

You'll need:

- 13 Basket Blocks finishing to 10"
- 8 Edge Triangles
- 4 Smaller Corner Triangles
- 1-1/2" Inner Border
- 3" Outer Border

Fabric Requirements

- 2 yards of light background print. (If you want to vary the basket backgrounds buy 2 prints, 1-1/2 yards and 1 yard.)
- 1-1/2 yards of black and white stripe for outer border & two baskets
- 6 fat quarters of stripes for the 11 other baskets
- 1-1/2 yards of red for flowers and inner border
- 1 fat quarter of yellow for the appliqué if you haven't enough scraps
- 3 fat quarters of green for the appliqué
- 1/2 yard black for the binding

Cutting

We give you rotary cutting instructions below and templates for the block (there is no template for A.)

Blocks

Baskets

A- Cut a 10 7/8" square of background fabric. Cut into 2 triangles diagonally. You need one triangle per block.

Fig. 8.13

B – Cut a 12 1/2" strip of 5/8" bias or use template

C – Cut a 6 7/8" square of striped fabric. Line the stripes up on the bias. Cut in half diagonally to make 2 triangles. You need one per block. see illus # 8.10

D – Cut a 2 7/8 "square of striped fabric. Line the stripes up on the bias. Cut in half diagonally to make 2 triangles. You need 2 per block.

E – Cut two rectangles of background fabric 6 7/8" x 2 1/2". Trim the 45 degree angles. Or use template

F – Cut a 4 7/8" square of background fabric. Cut in half diagonally to make 2 triangles. You need one per block.

Appliqué Florals

Cut pieces using the templates, adding a bit under 1/4" for the seam allowance.

Edge Triangles

■ For the sides: Cut 2 squares 15 3/8" of background fabric. Cut each into 4 triangles. You'll need 8 large triangles. (Note: These finish the same size as piece A, but the grain line runs the other way, so you'll be cutting them differently)

■ For the Corners: Cut 2 squares 8" of background fabric. Cut each into 2 triangles. You'll need 4 smaller triangles. Trim these to fit.

Borders

Jean did not miter the borders but used shorter strips on the top and bottom. If you would prefer to miter the borders, cut 4 of the longer strips.

Inner Border (finishes to 1-1/2")

■ Cut 2 strips 2" x 43" of red for the top & bottom

■ Cut 2 strips 2" x 46" of red for the sides

Outer Border (finishes to 3")

■ Cut 2 strips 3-1/2" x 46" of stripes for top & bottom

■ Cut 2 strips 3-1/2" x 53" of stripes for the sides

Stitching the Blocks

See instructions on page 93.

Setting the Quilt

Set the blocks side by side in diagonal strips with triangles finishing each strip as shown.

Borders

■ Add the top and bottom red border; then the sides.

■ Press and trim, if necessary.

■ Add the top and bottom outer border, then the sides.

■ Press and trim, if necessary.

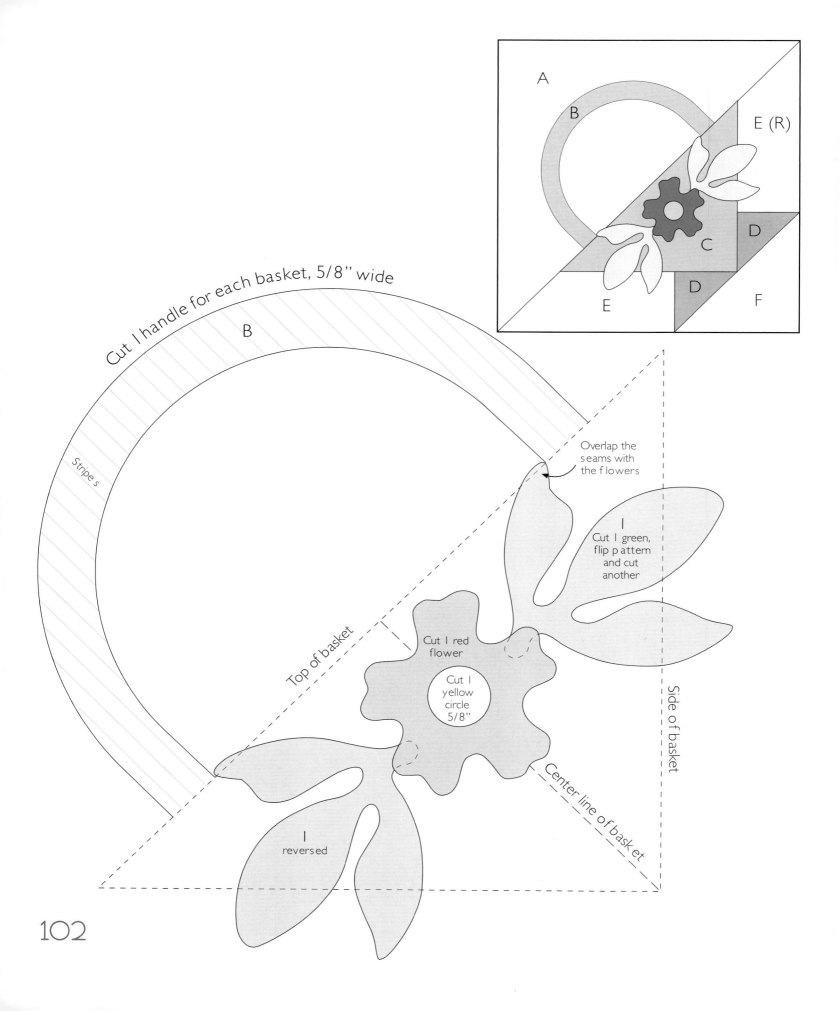

Cut I handle for each basket, 5/8" wide

B

Stripes

A

B

E (R)

C

D

D

E

F

Overlap the seams with the flowers

I
Cut I green, flip pattern and cut another

Top of basket

Cut I red flower

Cut I yellow circle 5/8"

Side of basket

Center line of basket

I reversed

102

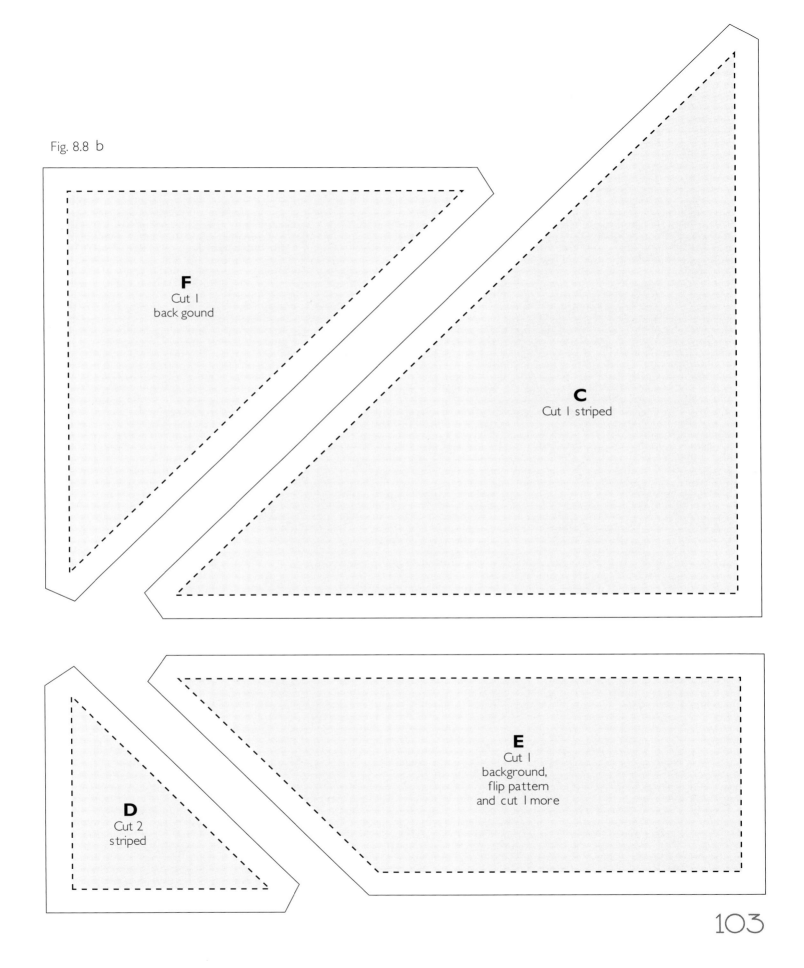

Fig. 8.8 b

F
Cut 1
back gound

C
Cut 1 striped

D
Cut 2
striped

E
Cut 1
background,
flip pattern
and cut 1 more

Susannah Christenson's vivid version of "Rose's Orchid" was photographed with publications featuring Rose Kretsinger's masterpieces. For a full view of Susannah's *Blessings in the Baskets* see page 165. The orchid is drawn from the Orchid Wreath pictured on the dust jacket of *The Romance of the Patchwork Quilt in America*. Above is a hand-drawn Kretsinger pattern with glued swatches for color suggestions.

Rose Kretsinger
Master Quiltmaker

Most of the influential quilt pattern designers working in the 1920s and '30s shared their patterns in print. Rose Kretsinger (1886-1963) of Emporia, Kansas, occasionally published one of her appliqué patterns in a magazine, but her great influence on Midwestern design was primarily through the old-fashioned method of tracing designs by hand and giving them to friends.

Rose Francis Good graduated from high school in Kansas City and went on to study design at the School of the Art Institute of Chicago, graduating in 1908. After a year in Europe she returned to Chicago and designed jewelry until she married an Emporia banker and retired from commercial art.

She was born in Hope, Kansas, southeast of Abilene. Her father, Milton Good, had been a partner in Good & Eisenhower, a dry goods store. Shortly before Rose's birth, he sold his share to David Eisenhower. When their new daughter was a few weeks old, Milton and Anna Good returned to Abilene. David Eisenhower, who could not make the store profitable, eventually moved to Texas,

where he and his wife, Ida, added a son named Dwight David Eisenhower to the family.

In her forties, while Rose's two children were growing, she began making quilts, first using patterns she found in magazines, then shaping her own variations of traditional appliqué updated with modern design flourishes. She earned local and national fame, wining prizes in quilt contests from the Lyon County Fair to New York City. Her national reputation grew with the 1935 book she co-wrote with Carrie Hall, *The Romance of the Patchwork Quilt in America.*

105

Rose's Orchid

Kretsinger had no formal pattern business with printed designs, but daughter Mary recalled that she was glad to draw patterns for friends and even strangers, charging $2.00 to $3.50 for full-sized appliqué and quilting patterns with small swatches of fabric attached. People in Emporia remembered her as generous with her patterns and her time. She'd help place a butterfly in a wreath or donate a scrap of her own favorite fabric to the project.

The quilting on Kretsinger's quilts is outstanding. Like so many of the quilts in this book, her masterpieces were a collaboration between the quiltmaker and a professional quilter. Rose designed the quilting patterns and marked the tops for a group of skilled hand quilters. Their specialty was an elaborate feather border flowing from fleur-de-lis placed in the corners. On page 110 we give you quilting designs adapted from one of her hand-drawn fleur-de-lis, drawn to fit in the two edge triangles that finish out the *Designer Basket* top.

Kretsinger's quilts are now in the collection of the Spencer Museum of Art at the University of Kansas. Many consider the *Orchid Wreath*, made in 1929, to be her masterpiece. When Mary asked for an orchid quilt to match her bedroom décor, Rose found inspiration in an advertising card she had seen at a soda fountain. The appliquéd orchid here is drawn from Rose's original design.

The traditional basket, called either "Cake Stand" or "Basket of Strawberries" is one her mother Anna Gleissner Good made about 1925.

Rotary Cutting the Basket

Piece K: Cut 9 7/8" squares of background fabric and the dark pink. Cut each in half diagonally. You'll need one triangle of each.
Piece L: Cut three 3 7/8" light squares of the background fabric. Cut four 3 7/8" squares of the dark pink. Cut each in half diagonally for a total of 14 triangles.
Piece M: Cut one 3 1/2" square of the background fabric.
Piece N: Cut one 6 7/8" square of the background fabric.
Piece O: Cut two 3 1/2 by 9 1/2" rectangles of the background.

Stitching the Basket

Piece the basket block first. Then appliqué the orchid on top of the seams.

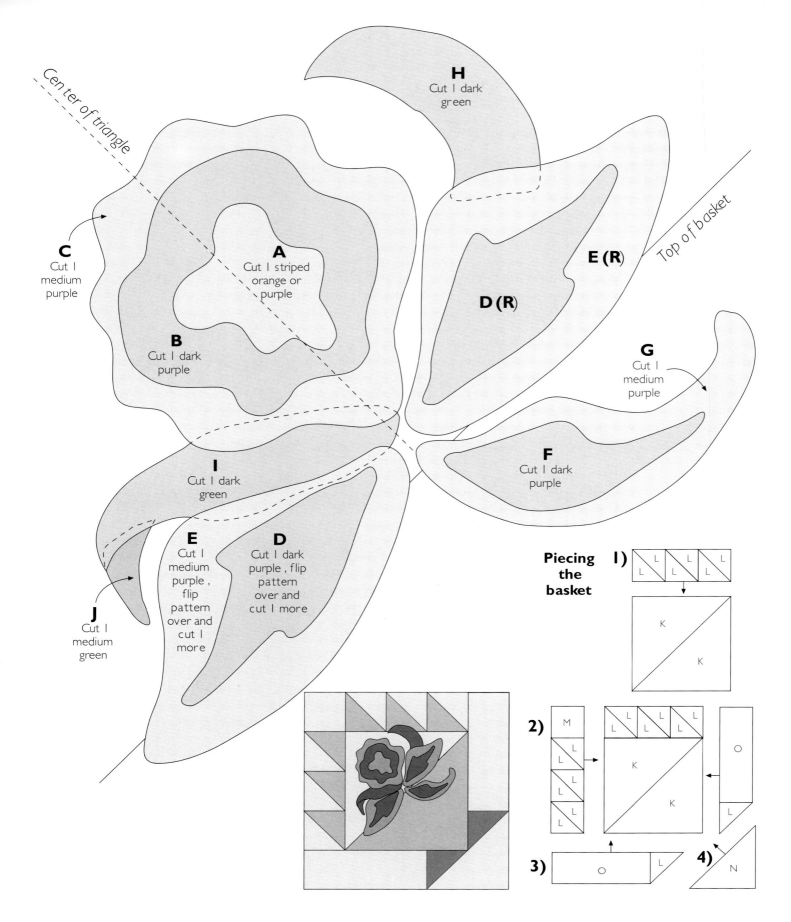

H
Cut 1 dark
green

Center of triangle

C
Cut 1
medium
purple

A
Cut 1 striped
orange or
purple

B
Cut 1 dark
purple

E (R)

Top of basket

D (R)

G
Cut 1
medium
purple

I
Cut 1 dark
green

F
Cut 1 dark
purple

E
Cut 1
medium
purple,
flip
pattern
over and
cut 1
more

D
Cut 1 dark
purple, flip
pattern
over and
cut 1 more

J
Cut 1
medium
green

**Piecing
the
basket**

1)

L	L	L
L	L	L

K

K

2)

| M |
| L |
| L |
| L |

L	L	L
L	L	L

K

K

O

L

3)   O   L

4)   N

108

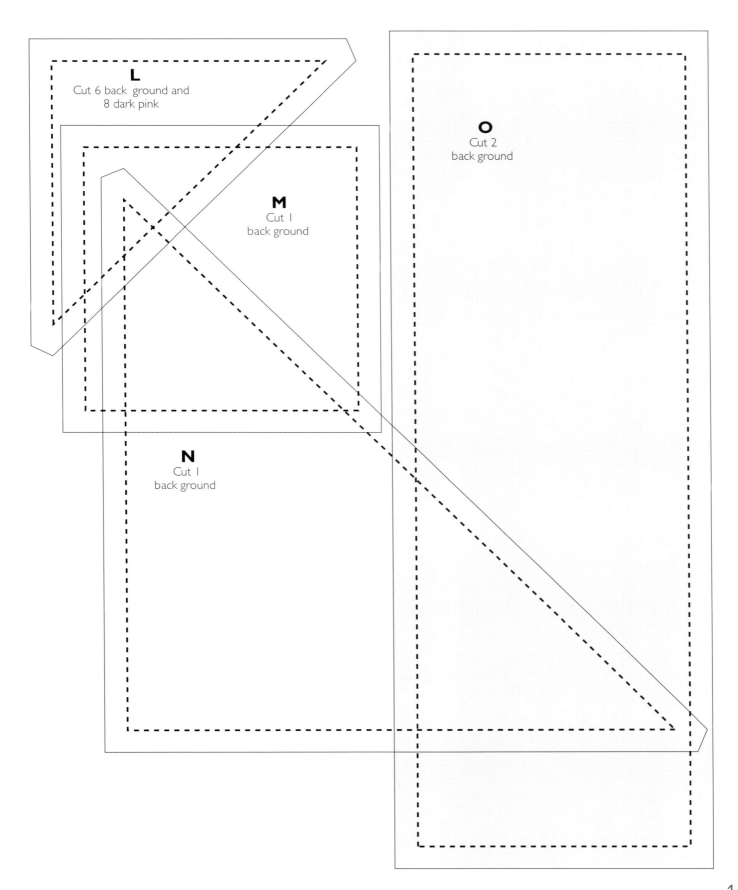

L
Cut 6 back ground and
8 dark pink

M
Cut 1
back ground

N
Cut 1
back ground

O
Cut 2
back ground

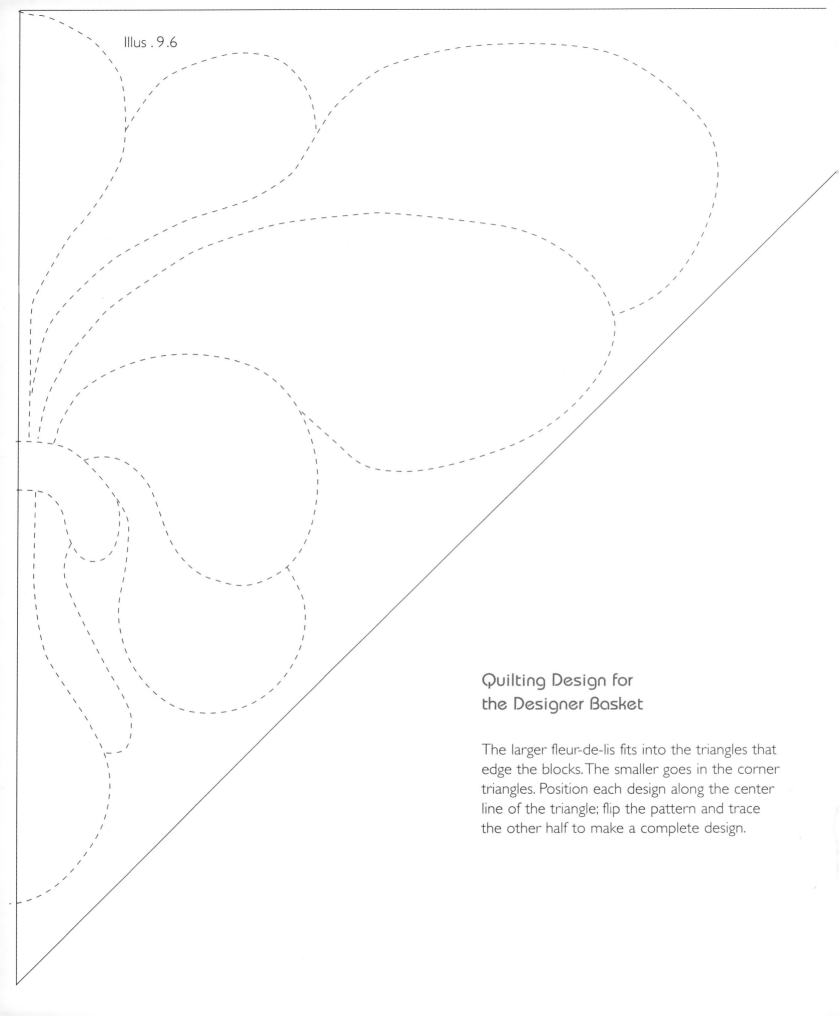

Illus . 9.6

Quilting Design for the Designer Basket

The larger fleur-de-lis fits into the triangles that edge the blocks. The smaller goes in the corner triangles. Position each design along the center line of the triangle; flip the pattern and trace the other half to make a complete design.

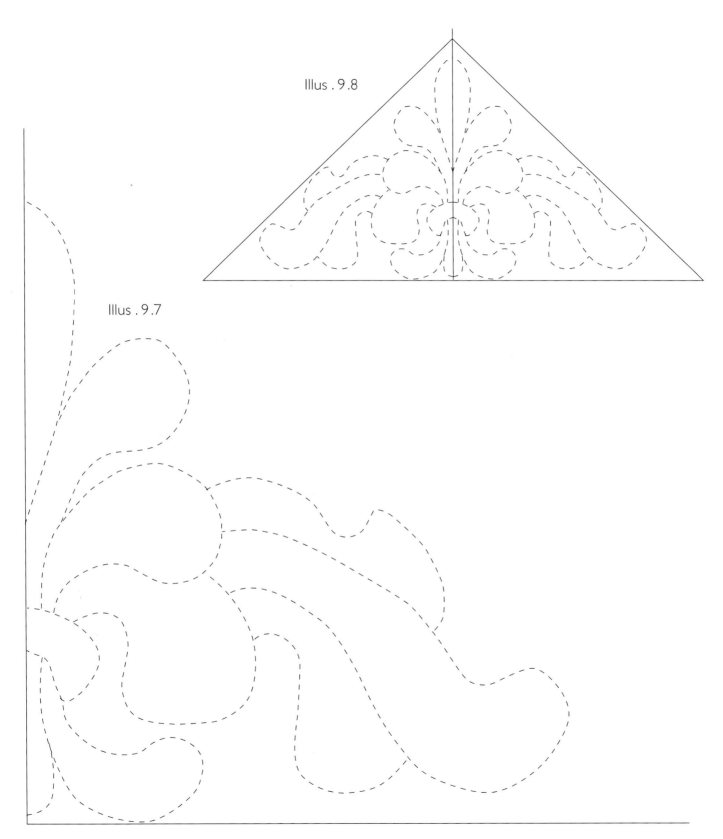

Illus . 9.8

Illus . 9.7

111

Shirley and Shirlene Wedd used the colors of nature for their basket sampler (see page 165). On the right is a page from Hall and Kretsinger's *Romance of the Patchwork Quilt in America*. Above a photo of Madam Hall, about 1935, dressed in a "Colonial" costume she wore for her lectures. The word "Colonial" was a catch-all for 1930's nostalgia. Figures mixed costumes with Civil-War hoop skirts and mob-caps from Martha Washington's time to lend a "Colonial" touch to everything from match holders to sachet pillows.

Carrie Hall
Quilt Pattern Collector

Rather than drawing quilt patterns for the newspapers, Carrie Hall of Leavenworth, Kansas, was an avid reader of the pattern columns. She collected the clippings with the initial hope, she once wrote, of making a quilt in every printed design. Facing the numbers - thousands of published quilt designs - she soon decided that stitching a single block in each pattern was a more practical goal. Again, her objective was too ambitious, but she finished about 850 pieced and appliquéd blocks before abandoning the project in the mid-1930s.

Carrie Alma Hackett (1866-1955) was born in Wisconsin and came to Kansas as a child, growing up in Smith Center. As a young woman hoping to support herself as a dressmaker, she moved to Leavenworth, a prosperous city dominated by the Army's Staff College where officers spent extended stays accompanied by their well-dressed wives. By the early 20th century, she was a respected dress designer known as Madam Hall.

Carrie married twice, first to Will Patterson, who died of a kidney ailment in 1903, and again to John Hall. She was a compulsive collector, gathering libraries about Shakespeare, costume, music and Abraham

Lincoln. As her collection of quilt blocks grew, she began lecturing about them to the many ladies' groups to which she belonged. After the stock market crash in 1929 when demand for elaborate hand-made clothing decreased, Hall turned her quilt hobby into a lecturing business

In 1935, Carrie published photographs of her blocks in the book *Romance of the Patchwork Quilt in America*, co-written with Rose Kretsinger. Hall claimed that she didn't write the book - "It wrote itself," a statement that appears to be quite true. Much of the text is copied directly from published sources, primarily the clippings she kept in her scrap

Madam Hall's Colonial Basket

books. She did little original research into patterns, pattern names or the history of quilting. Her major talent was as an organizer of the large amount of material she'd collected. For many years, the book served as the best index to pattern names for quilters and collectors. Many of today's long-term quiltmakers drew their first patterns from Hall's tiny black and white photos.

Hall's sources were the many magazine and newspaper columns of the years 1910-1935 - patterns, catalogs from Carlie Sexton, Ruby McKim and Aunt Martha, clippings from farm magazines and women's pages. She began collecting patterns soon after World War I, when she took up quiltmaking to fill the time she'd spent on the sewing that the Red Cross had requested for the war effort.

Hall's blocks are now in the collection of the Spencer Museum of Art at the University of Kansas. Among the many newspaper designs are a few that appear to be originals, including the bouquet of iris and sunflowers adapted for "Madam Hall's Colonial Basket." The basket is drawn from one she called "Colonial Basket." No Colonial seamstress ever made a quilt in such a pattern (most pre-Revolutionary War quilts were of whole cloth rather than patchwork), but romance was at the heart of Carrie Hall's imagination. Names like "Colonial Basket" and Madam Hall spoke of far more interesting times and places than Dust Bowl Kansas.

Rotary Cutting the Basket

Piece G: Cut a 15 7/8" square of the background fabric. Cut in half diagonally to make two triangles. You'll need one.

Piece H: Cut squares 3 3/8". Cut three from light purple fabric and five from dark purple. Cut each in half diagonally to make two triangles. You'll need six light triangles and nine dark.

Piece I: Cut two rectangles 3" by 10 7/8" of the background fabric. Trim the 45 angles or use the template.

Piece J: Cut one rectangle 2 1/4" by 8 1/4" of the dark purple fabric. Trim the 45 degree angles or use the template.

Piece K: Cut one square of background fabric 5 7/8". Cut in half diagonally to make two triangles. You'll need one. (There is no template for G.)

Stitching the Basket

■ Piece the basket block first.
■ Then appliqué the flowers, positioning the sunflower on top of the seams.

Illus. 10.4a

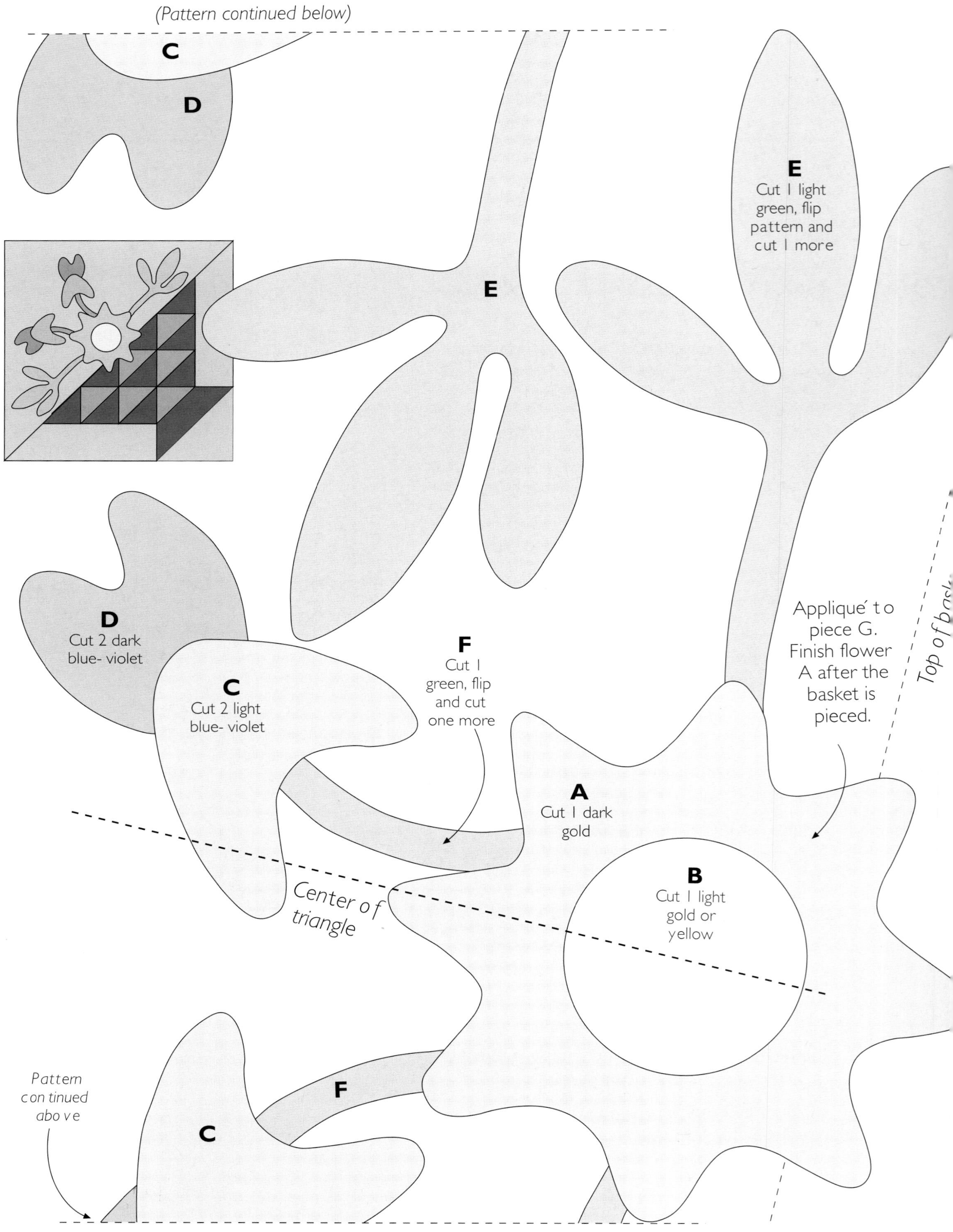

C

D

E
Cut 1 light
green, flip
pattern and
cut 1 more

E

D
Cut 2 dark
blue- violet

C
Cut 2 light
blue- violet

F
Cut 1
green, flip
and cut
one more

Appliqué t o
piece G.
Finish flower
A after the
basket is
pieced.

Top of bask

A
Cut 1 dark
gold

B
Cut 1 light
gold or
yellow

*Center of
triangle*

*Pattern
con tinued
abo v e*

C

F

Illus. 10.4b

Piecing the basket

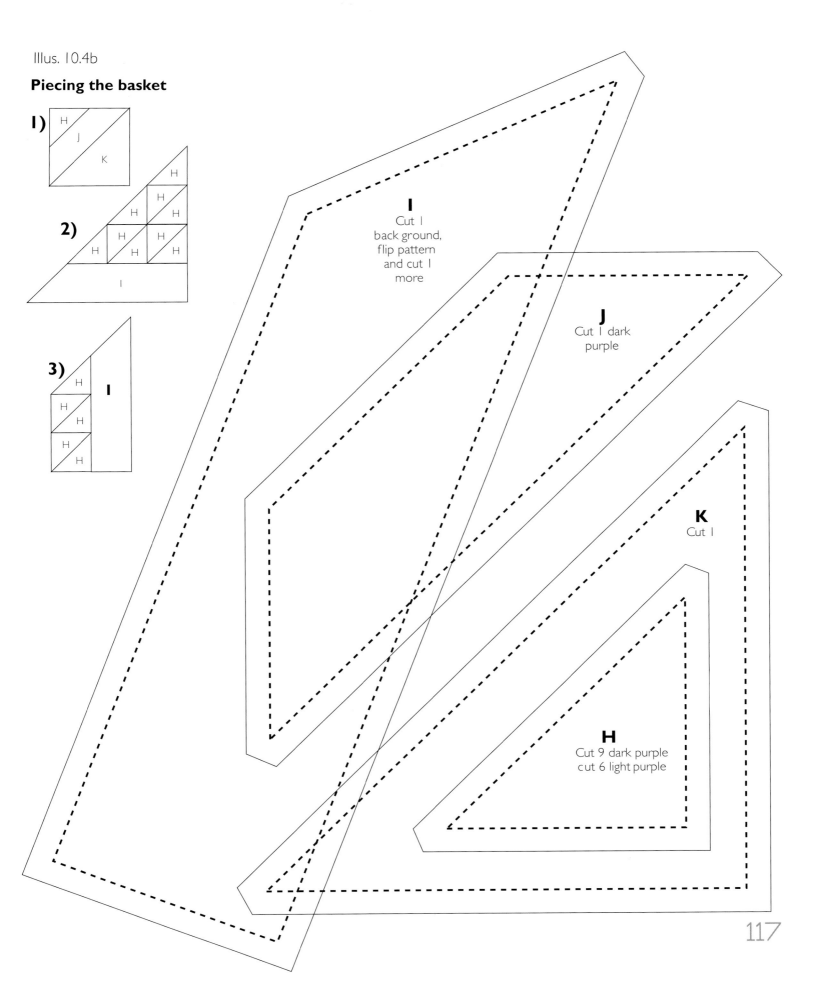

1)

2)

3)

I
Cut 1
back ground,
flip pattern
and cut 1
more

J
Cut 1 dark
purple

K
Cut 1

H
Cut 9 dark purple
cut 6 light purple

Lisa Gray's fine hand quilted rendition of "Kate's Wild Rose" is pictured with a black straw hat and a crocheted sachet case from Louise Fowler Roote's estate. On the right are the original drawings for quilts that appeared in *Capper's Weekly*.

Louise Fowler Roote
Newspaper Editor

AUTUMN LEAF, BLUE-RIBBON QUILT AT STATE FAIR

"Autumn Leaf"
was drawn from a prizewinner
at the Topeka State Fair in the early 1930s

Capper's Weekly, a periodical published in Topeka, Kansas, has for many years published quilt patterns. The first designs appeared in 1927 in the women's section, "The Heart of the Home." The fictional editor who supplied recipes, child raising advice and household hints was Kate Marchbanks, nom de plume for Louise Fowler Roote (1898-1987.)

Roote recalled that she began picturing quilt blocks because readers requested them. "I drafted my first pattern from a quilt mother was making - Hundreds of women put 15 cents in a letter for that pattern. From then on I had a new chore added to my other weekly duties - hunting for quilts, drafting their patterns - I haunted State Fairs, Quilting Bees and Teas."

Roote may have been the artist who actually drew the plates for the paper and the patterns to be mailed to readers. "By our present day standard of patterns those early ones of mine, done on the typewriter and mimeograph (the only means available) were pretty primitive... I had found a way to put to use the straight-A grades I had made in my college math courses. But I did have to smile as I recalled my old philosophy professor's sage comment, 'Now what good is trigonometry ever going to do a girl? It won't help her one iota when it comes to putting a triangle on a baby!'"

Kate's Wild Rose

In the mid-1930s, Roote began substituting syndicated patterns from Hubert Ver Mehren and the Aunt Martha companies for *Capper's Weekly's* original quilt column. She and her staff no longer had to search for antique designs, draft them and send copies to the readers. "Kate Marchbanks" may have been happy to turn those tasks over to the syndicates, but quilt historians regret that the local focus was lost. Topeka artists were no longer uncovering antique quilts in local collections or developing unique designs.

In a short biography written in 1971, Louise testified, "I was never really born - I just hatched out in a desk drawer in the old Capper Publications building." According to Social Security records, however, she was born on Christmas Day, 1898 in Kansas. She attended Topeka's Washburn University and then worked at *Capper's Weekly* for her entire career, serving first as women's page editor and then general editor after 1943.

The "Cherry Basket" here is a classic basket design pieced of quite a few half square triangles, a rather ambitious project published in 1938. The simple floral appliqué was inspired by a modern design from the "Heart of the Home" page, possibly a Roote original.

Rotary Cutting the Basket

Piece D: Cut a 15 7/8" square of the background fabric. Cut in half diagonally to make 2 triangles. You'll need one.

Piece E: Cut squares 2 3/4". Cut 10 from dark gold fabric and 8 from light gold or yellow. Cut each in half diagonally to make 2 triangles. You'll need 20 dark and 15 light triangles.

Piece F: Cut 2 rectangles 2 3/8" by 12 1/8" of the background fabric. Trim the 45 degree angles or use the template.

Piece G. Cut 1 rectangle 1 7/8" by 6 1/2" of the dark gold fabric. Trim the 45 degree angles or use the template.

Piece H: Cut 1 square of background 4 5/8". Cut in half diagonally to make 2 triangles. You'll need 1. (There is no template for D.)

Stitching

■ Piece the basket block first.
■ Then appliqué the flowers, positioning the leaf on top of the seams.

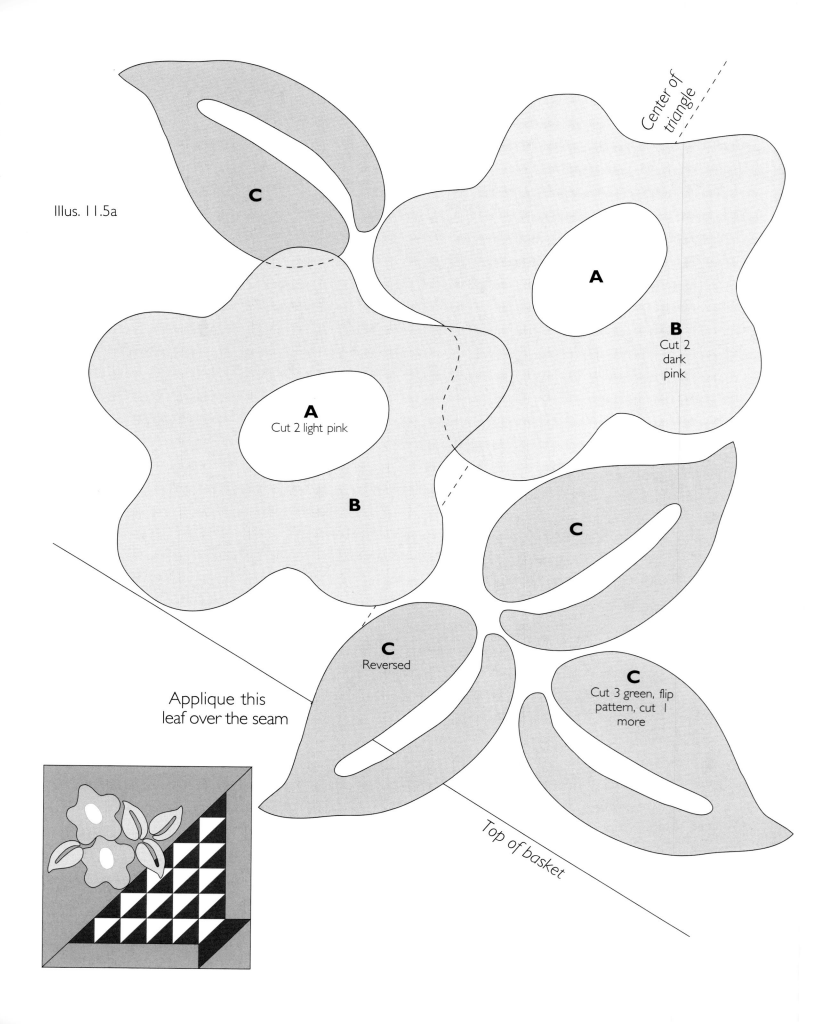

Illus. 11.5a

C

A
Cut 2 light pink

B

A

B
Cut 2
dark
pink

Center of triangle

C

C
Reversed

C
Cut 3 green, flip pattern, cut 1 more

Applique this leaf over the seam

Top of basket

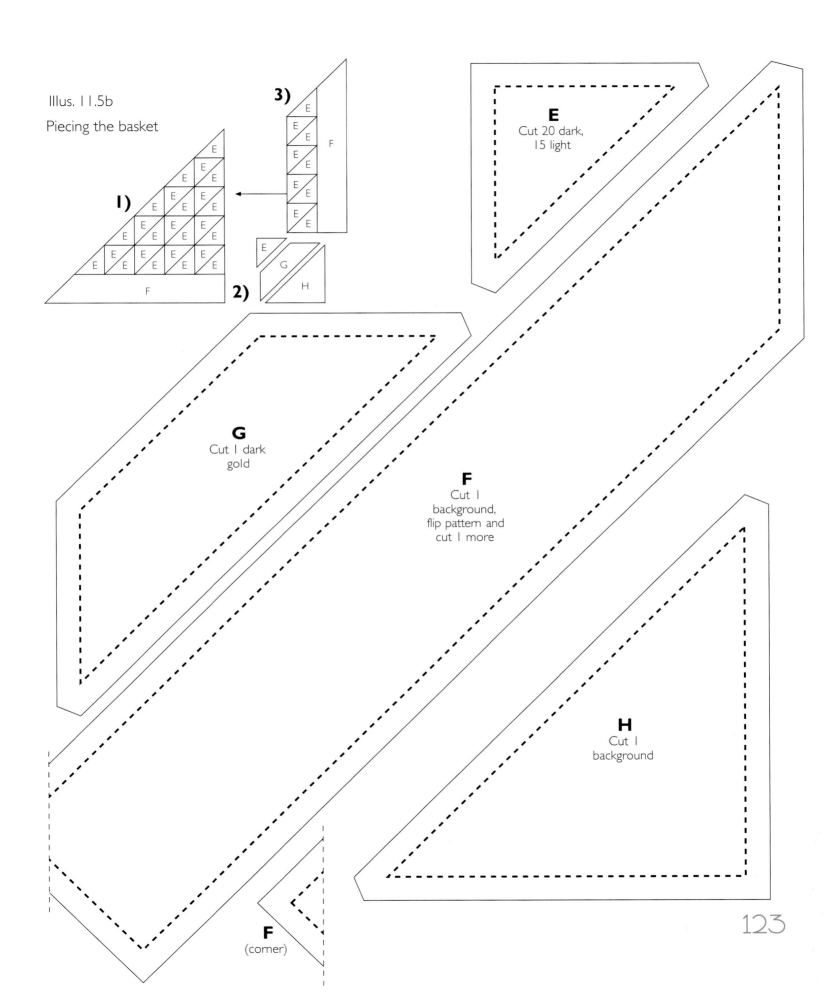

Illus. 11.5b

Piecing the basket

1)

2)

3)

E
E E
E E E
E E E E
E E E E E
E E E E E E
F

E
E
E
E
E
E
F

E
G
H

E
Cut 20 dark,
15 light

G
Cut 1 dark
gold

F
Cut 1
background,
flip pattern and
cut 1 more

H
Cut 1
background

F
(corner)

The Basket of Good Cheer" is positively perky when pieced in polka dots as in this version by Deb Rowden. For another view of her quilt, *Lotsa Dots*, see page 166. Note that Deb added extra dots in the sashing by appliquéing circles. On the top left is a set of old feedsack dishtowels, fancied up with dots of varying sizes. Many collectors who clipped the quilt columns from the newspaper organized them into scrapbooks. The two old composition books on the right are bursting with patterns. At the bottom, a tin quilting template.

Oklahoma Farmer Stockman
Rural Resource

The Weekly Star Farmer was The Star's sister newspaper published for the agricultural market in the Midwest. Farm wives expected quilt patterns in their periodicals and for decades The Star duplicated the pattern from Sunday's city paper in Wednesday's Star Farmer (also called for a time the Weekly Kansas City Star.)

Periodicals giving news and advice to farmers date to the early nineteenth century. Agricultural papers thrived as printing technology improved, paper became cheaper, the farming population increased and mail rates dropped. It's estimated that ninety farm periodicals were published in 1870, a number that doubled in the next decade. The journals were generally regional in scope with a New England Farmer, a Rural New Yorker and a Western Farm Journal catering to different climate, crops and politics. Competition dictated features for the family and many magazines had a women's page with household hints and needlework patterns.

Farm families on the Great Plains could subscribe to a variety of agricultural periodicals, among them the Oklahoma Farmer Stockman. The weekly included an original quilt pattern feature on their homemaking page, which was titled "Good Cheer." In the 1920s and early '30s, the patterns that appeared in the paper were mailed to the editors by readers from Kansas, Oklahoma and Texas, indicating the range of households reached by the paper.

Unique pattern columns such as the Good Cheer feature are valuable to quilt pattern collectors because they recorded regional names and designs. In 1921, a woman from Kiowa County, Oklahoma, sent "The Hog Pen," a log cabin variation more commonly known as "Court House Steps." That local name was never recorded in the big city publications, possibly because "Hog Pen" was considered too folksy, too rural, too low-brow for a more sophisticated audience. Many of the regional subscribers, however, must have recognized the down-to-earth name.

Basket of Good Cheer

About 1935, the Good Cheer column changed from one offering readers' contributions to a nationally syndicated feature by Helen Kaufman, who wrote for numerous farm periodicals at the time. Helen's quilt patterns were also published in German-language publications directed at German-American farm families, many of whom were enthusiastic quilters. A woman with a name like Kaufman was probably able to write about quilts in German as well as English, or her editors may have translated her columns for their readers.

The basket here, "The Basket of Good Cheer," was published as "Cactus Pot" in 1930, probably sent in by a reader. The flowers were inspired by a Helen Kaufman design called "Blue Bells" from 1935.

Many of the women's pages offered fashion patterns as well as needlework and quilting designs

Rotary Cutting the Basket

Piece G: Cut 3 squares 8 3/8 inches, one of light green, one of dark green and one of background. Cut in half diagonally to make two triangles. You'll need one triangle of light, one dark and one background.

Piece H: Cut one square 4 1/4 inches of background fabric.

Piece I: Cut squares 4 5/8 inches. Cut one of dark green, two of light green and two of background fabric. Cut each in half diagonally to make two triangles. You'll need two dark green, four light green and four background triangles.

Piece J: Cut two rectangles 4 1/4 inches by 8 inches of background fabric.

Stitching

■ Piece the basket block first, leaving the center seam between the background and the basket pieces "G" open.

■ Insert the leaves and the stem in that open seam. Then stitch it closed.

■ Appliqué the flowers, leaves and stem, as shown, over the seams.

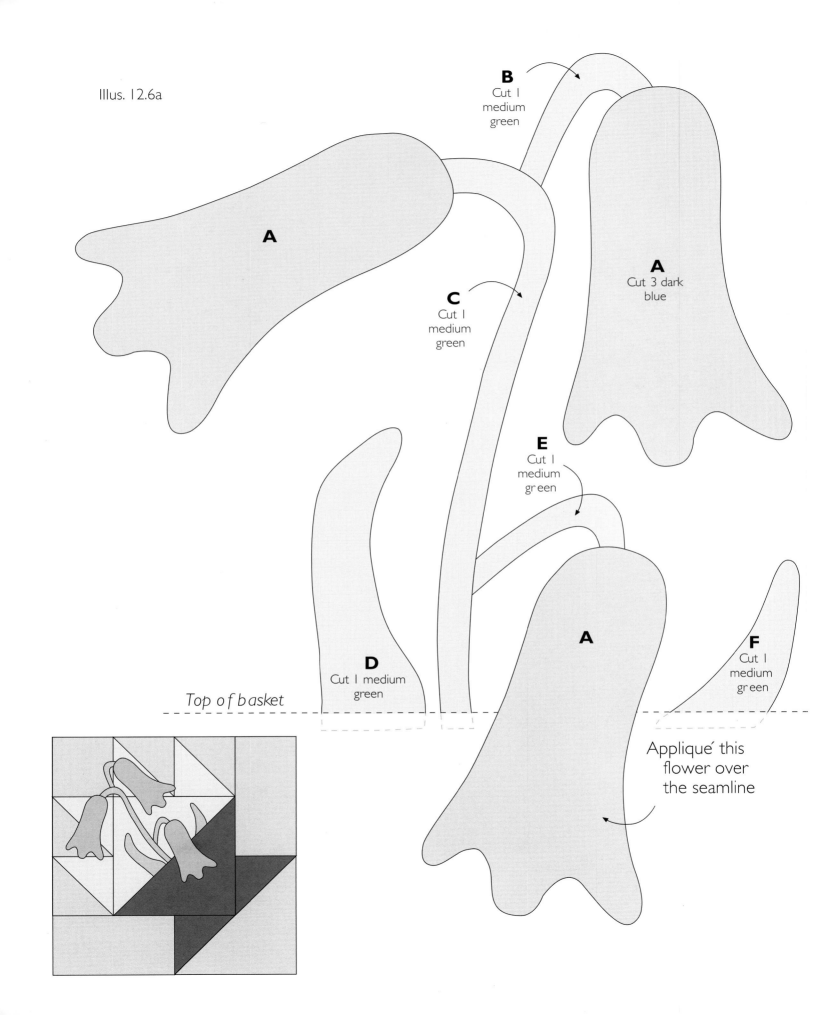

Illus. 12.6a

B
Cut 1
medium
green

A

A
Cut 3 dark
blue

C
Cut 1
medium
green

E
Cut 1
medium
green

D
Cut 1 medium
green

Top of basket

A

F
Cut 1
medium
green

Appliqué this
flower over
the seamline

Illus. 12.6b

Piecing the basket

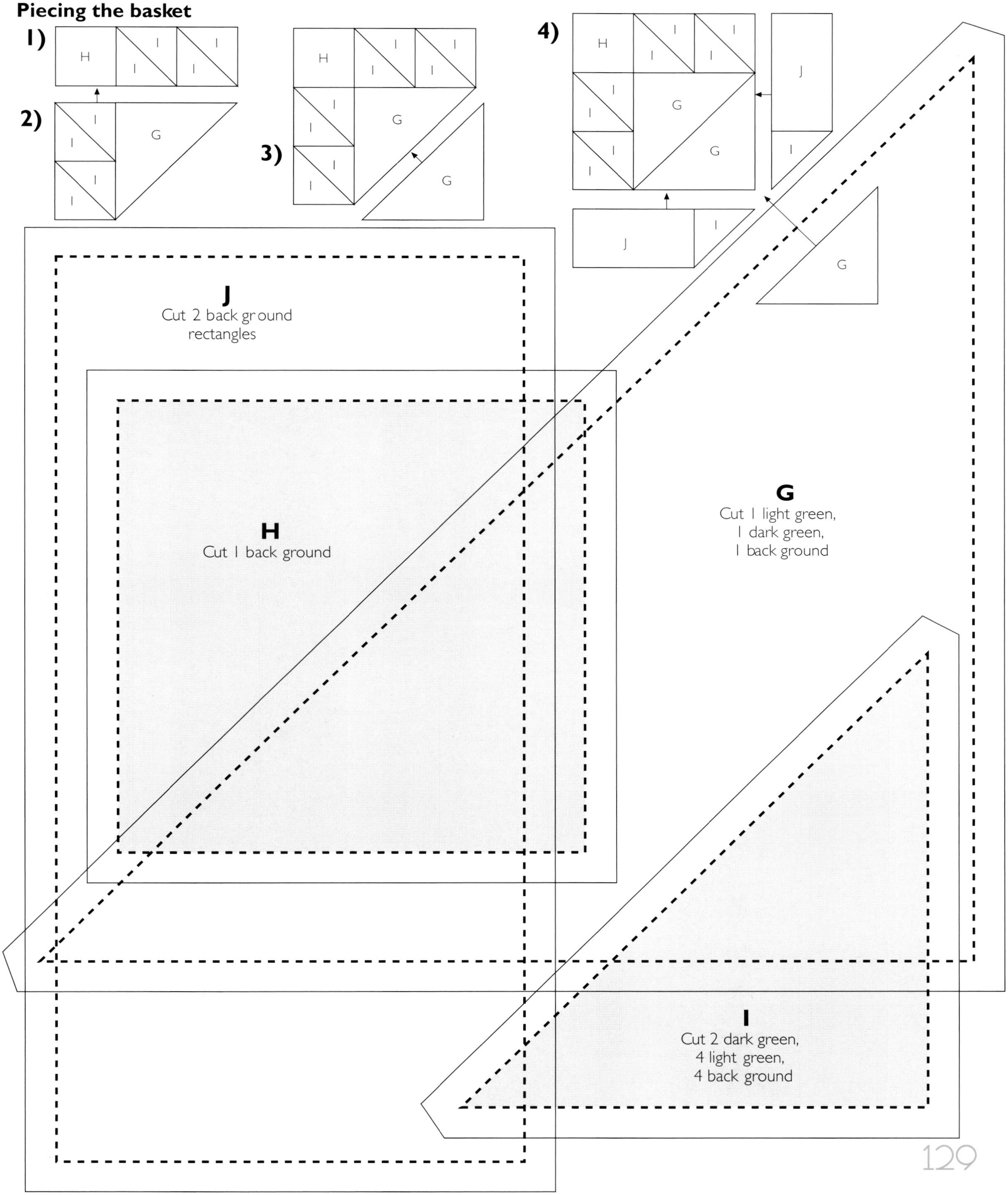

1)

2)

3)

4)

J
Cut 2 background
rectangles

H
Cut 1 background

G
Cut 1 light green,
1 dark green,
1 background

I
Cut 2 dark green,
4 light green,
4 background

129

Kathy Delaney's "Mrs. Danner's Lily" incorporates colorful reproduction prints with red and black plain fabrics. For a full view of Kathy's *Red Hot Women of Design* see page 158. Helen Ericson of Emporia, Kansas, reprinted many of Mrs. Danner's pattern pamphlets in the 1970s and added a few catalogs of her own.

Scioto Danner
Quilt Impresario

Scioto Danner ran a prosperous quilt pattern business in El Dorado, Kansas, during the heyday of the mid-twentieth century fad for patchwork. In the late 1920s, she and her mother began selling quilts, arranging with the Innes Department Store in Wichita to exhibit sample blocks and finished quilts. Few customers were interested in buying the quilts, she later recalled, but "so many people asked me for my designs that I took orders and came home and cut patterns by hand for those who wanted them so badly." Her dilemma: Should she sell the patterns people requested or should she reserve the designs for her finished quilts? She tried selling patterns at the Kansas State Fair and was so pleased with the demand that she revised her business plan.

Mrs. Danner's Quilts evolved from those first department store exhibits. Between 1920 and 1936 she traveled the country displaying quilts at regularly scheduled spring and fall showings. She hired six employees to travel the circuit, each selling finished quilts, blocks, basted tops, kits, and, most profitably, the patterns for women to make their own quilts.

Scioto Imhoff (1891-1974) was born in Carroll County, Missouri. Her unusual first name derives from Ohio's Scioto River. Her father had counted on a boy he planned to name Grover Cleveland, so no girl's name had been chosen. After six months as "the baby," she was named Scioto for the engraving inside a gold ring sent as a present. She pronounced her name Sie'-oh-toe," with all the vowels long and the emphasis on the first syllable, according to Helen Ericson, who bought Mrs. Danner's Quilts in the 1970s.

As a child, Scioto learned to sew and to love quilts. She attended high school in Plattsburg, Missouri, and the Teacher's College in Warrensburg. Her first career was as a schoolteacher in the towns of Sibley, Henrietta and Buckner, all in western Missouri. In 1917, when she was in her mid-twenties, she traveled to Maui, Hawaii, to teach for two years at the Maunaolu Seminary for girls. There she caught amoebic dysentery, which eventually forced her to retire from school teaching after her last position at Manchester School in Kansas City.

In 1927, she married Mr. Danner and moved to Texas, but the marriage lasted only a year or two. By the late 1920s, living with her parents in El Dorado, she turned to quilt patterns for an income. After making her first few quilts, Scioto did little sewing herself. In 1934, she told a reporter for *The Kansas City Star* that 24 women stitched her models. Her annual profit reached the four figures, "a fine income for mother and daughter." Over the years, she hung exhibits in 87 cities, including Kansas City, learning by experience that cities with fewer than 100,000 inhabitants would not turn a profit.

By 1936, Scioto was exhausted. She sold her quilt models, moved to Berkeley, California, where she managed a boarding house and rejected any mail orders as "refused." But following World War II, she returned to El Dorado and the quilt business, focusing on mail order patterns rather than traveling. In 1954 she wrote, "I sometimes think it would be fun to 'be a mouse,' as we say, after a couple of generations when the young matrons of 1990 or 2000 begin looking for their great-grandmother's quilts." She surely would have been pleased to see today's fascination with those antique quilts.

"Mrs. Danner's Lily" is adapted from a basket Scioto called "Red Basket." The floral appliqué is drawn from her "Centennial Lily," a design she copied from a fragment of an antique quilt to celebrate the hundredth anniversary of Kansas statehood in 1961.

Scioto Danner included small snapshots of quilts in her catalogs. This one, "The Irish Beauty," from her 1934 pamphlet *Mrs. Danner's Quilts,* is her original design based on traditional appliqué.

Mrs. Danner's Lily

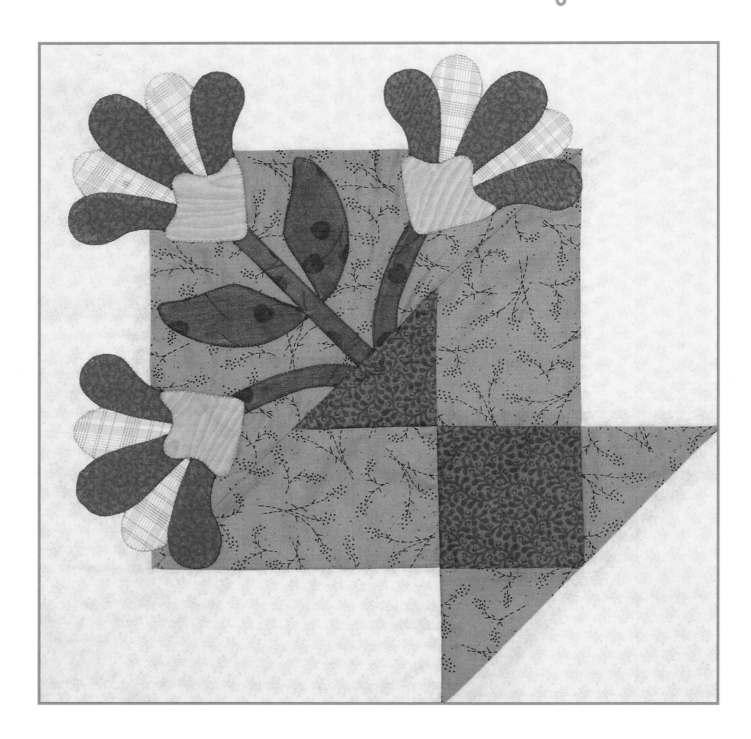

Rotary Cutting the Basket

Piece H: Cut one square 9 7/8" of light blue. Cut in half diagonally to make two triangles. You'll need one.

Piece I: Cut two rectangles of background fabric 16 1/4" by 3 1/2". Trim the 45 degree angles or use the template.

Piece J: Cut two rectangles of background fabric 9 7/8" by 3 1/2". Trim the 45 degree angles or use the template.

Piece K: Cut two rectangles of background fabric 6 7/8" by 3 1/2". Trim the 45 degree angles or use the template.

Piece L: Cut one square 3 1/2" of dark blue.

Piece M: Cut one square 3 7/8" of light blue and one of dark blue fabric. Cut each in half diagonally to make two triangles. You'll need two light triangles and one dark.

Piece N: Cut one square 6 7/8" of background fabric. Cut in half diagonally to make two triangles. You'll need one. (There are no templates for H, I, or N.)

Stitching

■ Piece the basket block first, leaving the center seam between the background piece "H" and the basket open.

■ Insert the stems in that open seam. Then stitch it closed.

■ Appliqué the flowers, leaves and stems, as shown, with the petals over the seams.

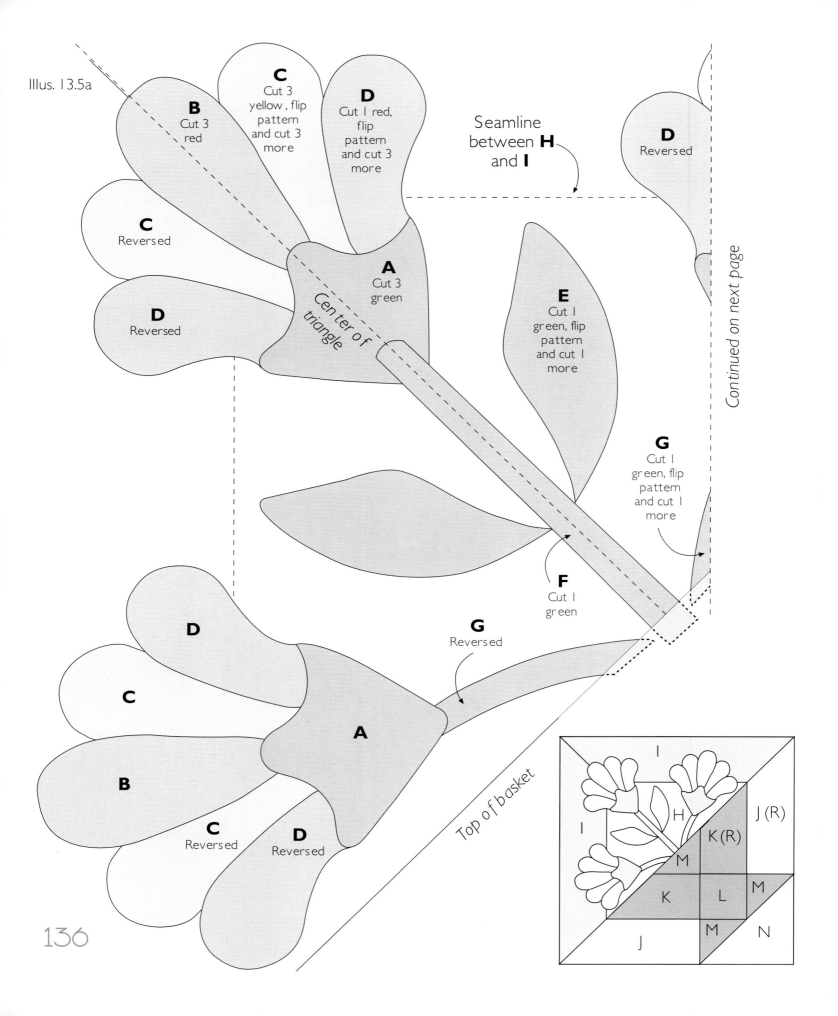

Illus. 13.5a

B Cut 3 red

C Cut 3 yellow, flip pattern and cut 3 more

D Cut 1 red, flip pattern and cut 3 more

Seamline between **H** and **I**

D Reversed

C Reversed

A Cut 3 green

Center of triangle

D Reversed

E Cut 1 green, flip pattern and cut 1 more

Continued on next page

G Cut 1 green, flip pattern and cut 1 more

F Cut 1 green

D

G Reversed

C

A

Top of basket

B

C Reversed

D Reversed

136

I

I

H

J (R)

K (R)

M

K

L

M

J

M

N

Illus. 13.5b

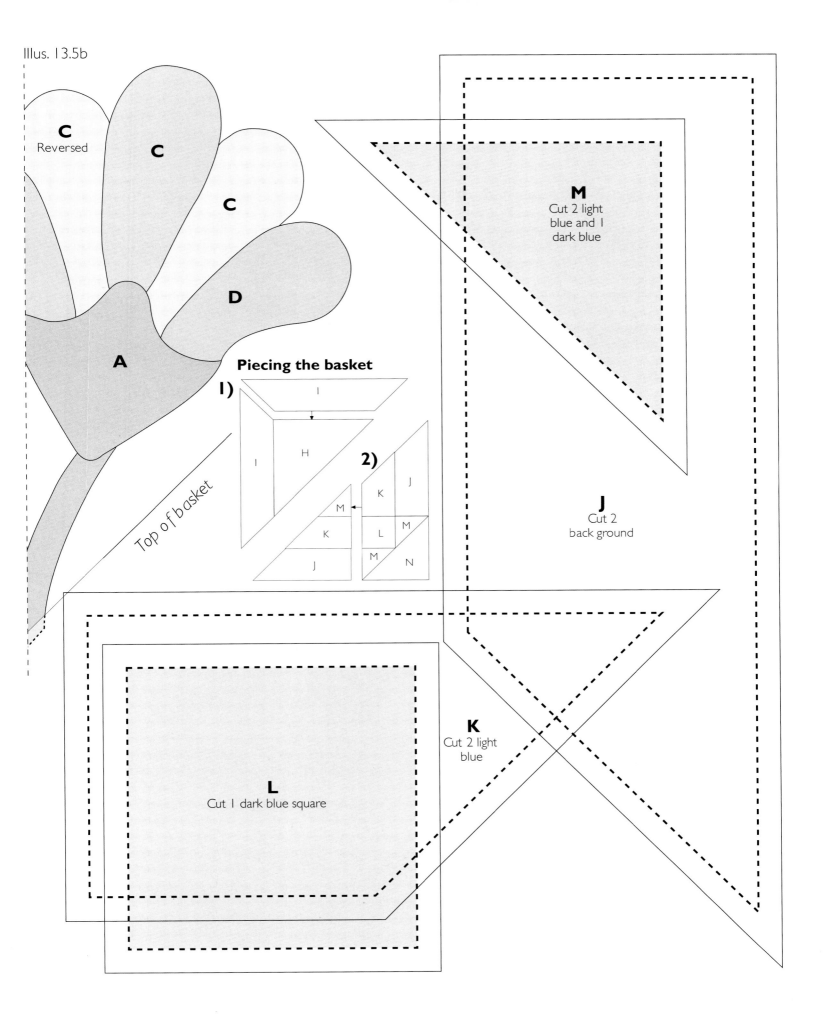

C Reversed

C

C

D

A

Piecing the basket

1)

I

I   H

Top of basket

2)

K   J

M

K   L   M

J   M   N

M
Cut 2 light
blue and 1
dark blue

J
Cut 2
back ground

K
Cut 2 light
blue

L
Cut 1 dark blue square

Christmas Baskets by Nancy P. Wakefield, Platte City, Missouri, 82 "x 82 ". Machine quilted by Linda Harker. Nancy picked subtle Christmas colors to stitch flowers of red and green in tan baskets. Her quilt is at home in any season, a good match for today's country decorating taste.

Sets & Borders for the Designer Basket

Christmas Baskets

82" Quilt

2" Sashing

5" Border

Nancy Wakefield's *Christmas Baskets* is sashed in simple fashion with a mitered, striped border. Below are instructions for her setting and border.

You'll Need:

- 13 blocks finishing to 15"
- 8 large triangles for the sides along the edge
- 4 medium triangles for the corners
- 36 sashing strips
- 12 cornerstones
- 12 small triangles to finish out the sashing
- 4 border strips

Fabric Requirements

- 2 yards of dark print for the sashing strips and binding
- 1 1/4 yards of background for the edge triangles
- 1/4 yard of green print for the cornerstones (cut fat or long)
- 2 1/2 yards of red stripe for the border
- 8 yards of backing to piece into a back

Cutting

- Cut 36 sashing strips 15 1/2" by 2 1/2" of the red print.
- Cut 12 cornerstone squares 2 1/2" of green print.
- For the smallest green triangles, cut 3 squares 3 3/4" and cut each in half diagonally with 2 lines to give you 12 triangles in all.
- For the large edge triangles, cut 2 squares of background 22 1/2". Cut each in half diagonally with 2 lines to give you 8 triangles in all.
- For the medium edge triangles, cut 2 squares of background 11 1/2". Cut each in half diagonally once to give you 4 triangles in all.
- For the borders, cut 4 strips 83" x 5 1/2" with the long side along the selvage edges of the stripe. Be sure you cut the same sequence of stripes for each strip so the mitered corners match up.

Setting the Quilt

- Set sashing strips between the blocks and edge triangles as shown below, alternating the strips of blocks with strips of sashing and cornerstones.
- Press the top and trim the edges.
- Add the borders, trim if necessary and miter the corners.

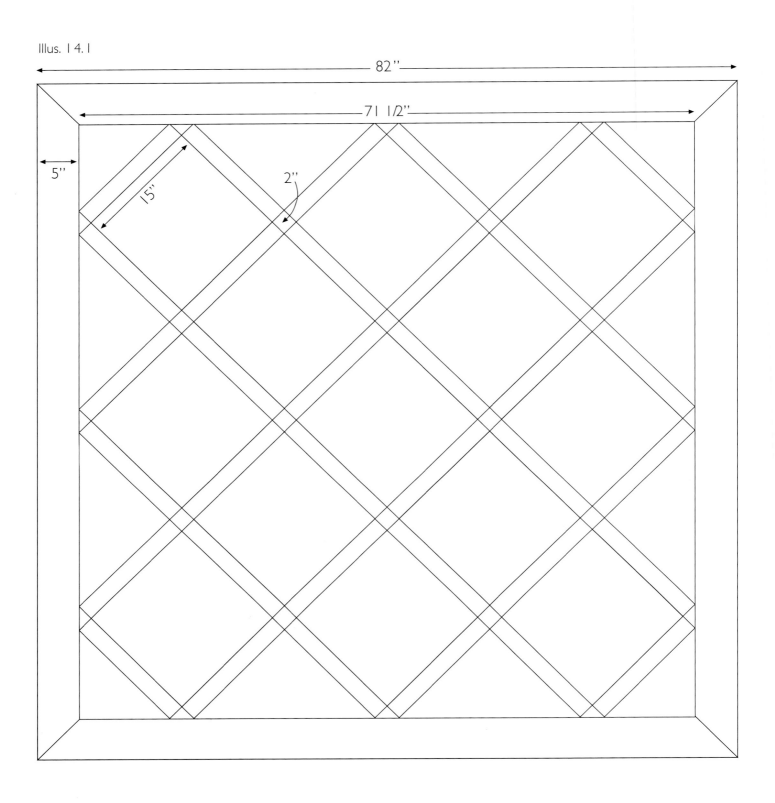

82"

71 1/2"

5"

15"

2"

Barbara's Baskets

Barbara's Baskets by Pat Moore, Kansas City, Missouri. 92" x 92". Machine quilted by Kelly Ashton. Pat chose a color scheme based on today's rather muted pastel prints, updating the mid-century look for her hand-appliquéd piece. Today's quilters love to insert a narrow border to frame the blocks. Her 1 1/2" green border that echoes the sashing adds to the contemporary look. The scalloped edge, however, is an old-fashioned touch, a finish that was quite popular in the 1930s for the very best quilts.

Barbara's Baskets

91" Quilt

2" Sashing

1 1/2" Inner Border

8" Scalloped Outer Border

You'll Need:

- 13 blocks finishing to 15"
- 8 large triangles for the sides along the edge
- 4 medium triangles for the corners
- 18 short sashing strips
- 6 longer sashing strips
- 4 border strips for the inner green border
- 4 border strips for the outer pink border

Fabric Requirements

- 1 1/4 yards of background for the edge triangles
- 2 1/2 yards medium green for sashing and inner border
- 4 yards large-scale pink print for outer border and binding
- 8 yards to piece together a backing

Cutting

- For the large edge triangles, cut 2 squares of background 22 1/2". Cut each in half diagonally with 2 lines to give you 8 triangles in all.
- For the medium edge triangles, cut 2 squares of background 11 1/2". Cut each in half diagonally once to give you 4 triangles in all.
- Cut 2 green strips 2" x 73" for the top and bottom borders (trim if necessary.)
- Cut 2 green strips 2" x 76 1/2" for the side borders (trim if necessary.)
- Cut 2 green sashing strips 2 1/2" x 88".
- Cut 2 green sashing strips 2 1/2" x 54".
- Cut 2 green sashing strips 2 1/2" x 20".
- Cut 18 green sashing strips 2 1/2" x 15 1/2".
- Cut 2 pink strips 8 1/2" x 76 1/2" for the top and bottom borders (trim later if necessary.)
- Cut 2 pink strips 8 1/2" x 93" for the side borders (trim later if necessary.)

Setting the Quilt

- Set sashing strips between the blocks and edge triangles as shown below, alternating the strips of blocks with strips of sashing.
- Press the top and trim the edges.
- Add the top and bottom green borders, then the sides.
- Press and trim the edges if necessary.
- Add the top and bottom pink borders, then the sides.
- Press and trim the edges if necessary.

Scalloping the Edge

Plan for the scalloped edge before you mark the top for quilting. Draw curves that cut in along the sides about 9 1/4" apart using a circle template (an old 33 1/3 record works well.) Be sure the quilting does not extend into the scallops.

- After the top is quilted, cut the curves.
- Bind with bias-cut strips, about 15 yards to account for the extra length required by the scallops.

Illus. 14.5

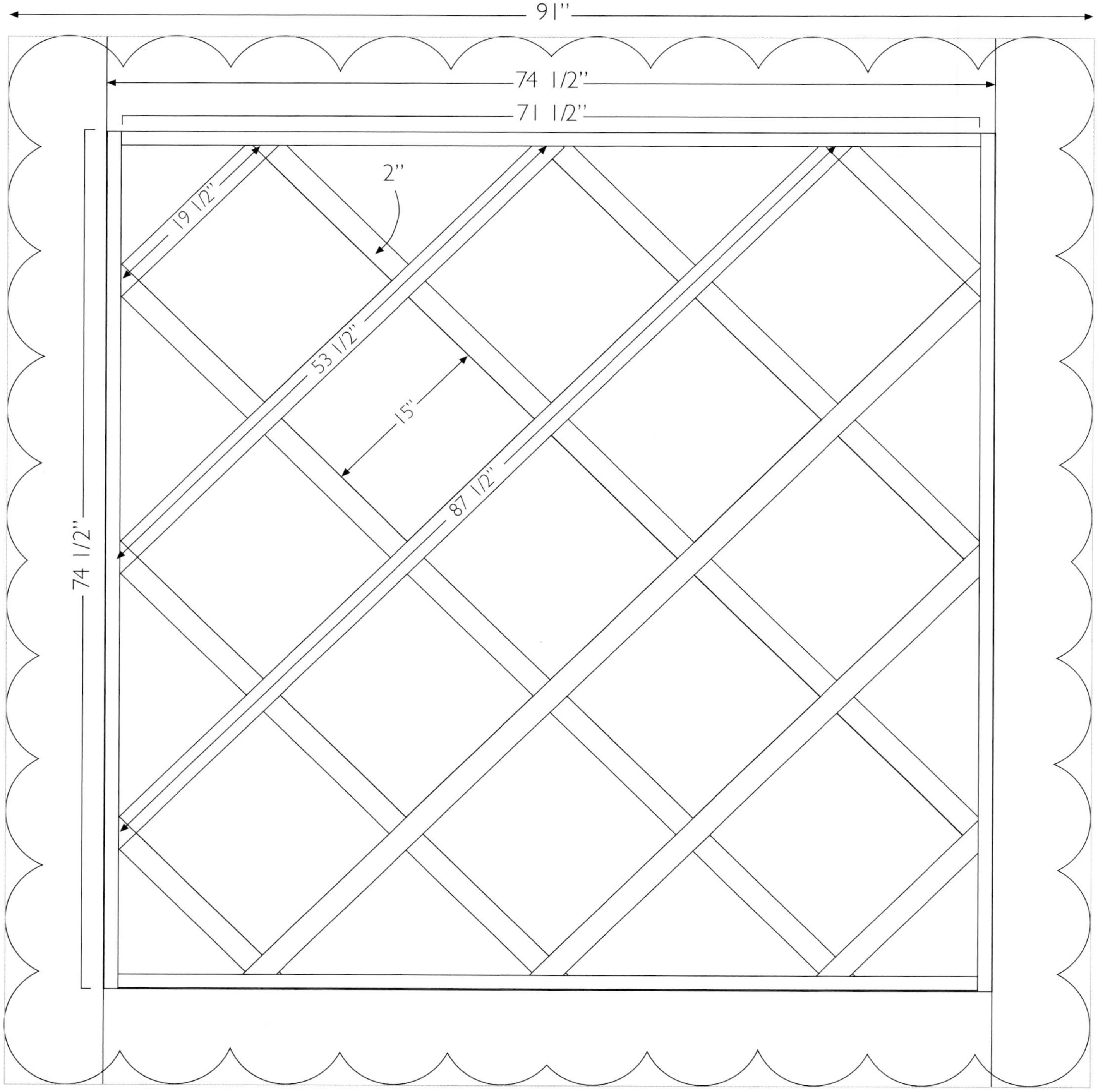
91"
74 1/2"
71 1/2"
2"
19 1/2"
53 1/2"
15"
87 1/2"
74 1/2"

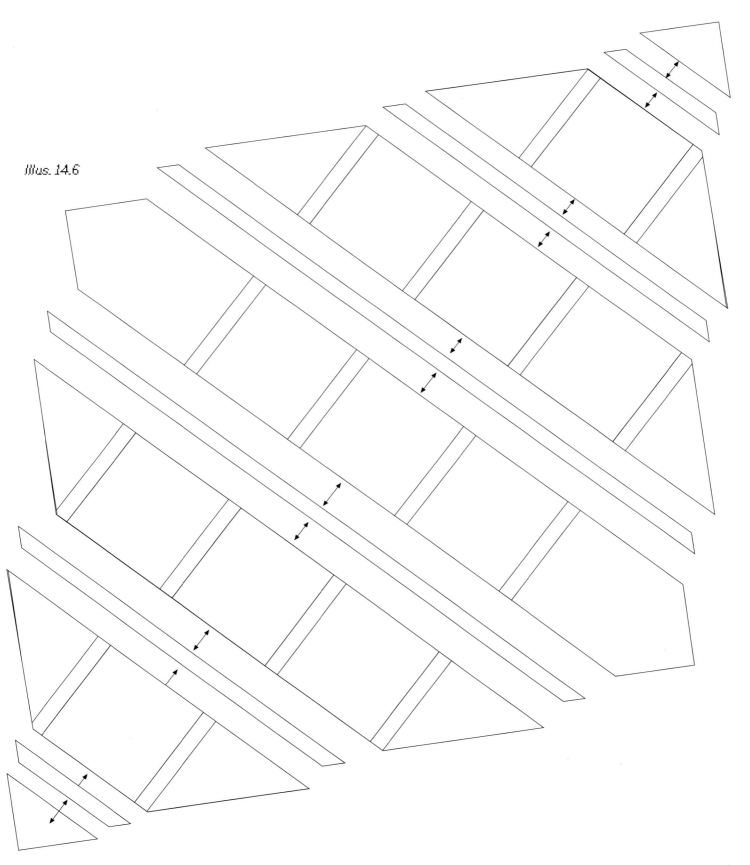

Illus. 14.6

From Another Time

73" Quilt
4 1/2" Pieced Border

You'll Need:

- 13 blocks finishing to 15"
- 8 large triangles for the sides along the edge
- 4 medium triangles for the corners
- 4 border strips 4 1/2" wide
- 4 cornerstones for the border 4 1/2"

Fabric Requirements

- 1 1/2 yard of ivory background for the edge triangles and the binding. (Notice that Kathy used a more yellow fabric for her edge. She wanted to echo the way the whites in antique quilts sometimes turn different yellows with age.)
- 6 quarter-yard pieces of prints (at least) for the piano key border or use fabric left over from the blocks to make it more scrappy looking.
- 4 yards of backing to piece together into a back

Cutting

- For the large edge triangles, cut 2 squares of background 22 1/2". Cut each in half diagonally with 2 lines to give you 8 triangles in all.
- For the medium edge triangles, cut 2 squares of background 11 1/2". Cut each in half diagonally once to give you 4 triangles in all.
- For the pieced border, cut 128 rectangles 2 1/2" by 5".
- For the cornerstones, cut 4 squares 5" by 5".

Piecing the Borders

- Piece together 4 strips of 32 rectangles each, varying the fabrics to give the scrappy look so popular mid-century.

Setting the Quilt

- Set diagonal strips of blocks and edge triangles as shown and then piece the strips together.
- Press the top and trim the edges.
- Add the top and bottom pieced borders. Note that the pieced border may be a little bit long so you will have to ease the seam so it fits or just trim the last rectangle to fit.
- Piece the 4 cornerstones to the ends of the side borders.
- Add the side borders, again easing if necessary.
- Press and trim the edges if necessary.

The appliquéd border here is adapted from a quilting pattern designed by the Aunt Martha company in the 1930s. The five-lobed flower is the common ditsy floral of the day. The simple border – a design that fit well in a newspaper column or an 8 1/2 by 11 sheet of mimeographed paper – is also typical of the time.

Designer Baskets

90" Quilt

2" Sashing

9" Appliquéd Border

Setting the Quilt

Set this quilt in the same fashion as the Christmas Baskets on page 138. The major difference is that the sashing strips are the same shade as the backgrounds in the blocks and the cornerstones are scraps of dark leftover from the blocks. The border here, which is not mitered, is wider.

Fabric Requirements for Setting & Border:

- 5 3/4 yards of background print for the sashing strips, the edge triangles and the border background
- 3/4 yard of dark for the cornerstones and binding (or use left over scraps and piece your binding)
- 5 yards of backing to piece into a back

You can use scraps left from the basket blocks or buy:

- 2/3 yard of green for the leaves
- 1/2 yard for the flowers (piece B)
- 1/4 yard for the floral centers (piece A)

Cutting the Border:

- For the top and bottom – 2 strips 9 1/2" x 72"
- For the sides – 2 strips 9 1/2" x 90 1/2"
- 24 border units of 1 flower and 2 leaves each.
- Plus 4 extra flowers for the corners.

Stitching:

■ Appliqué before you stitch your borders to the quilt.

■ Mark your border strips by pressing or using a removable marker.

■ On the top and bottom borders, which finish to almost 72", mark six 12 inch intervals as shown. These lines separate the border units. Because the border appliqué units are separate, you can fudge as you need to.

■ Do the same on the side borders leaving 9" squares at the ends. Remember to account for the 1/2 inch seam allowances as you mark.

■ Also mark a line that runs along the inside edge of each border 4 inches (actually 4 1/2" since you have to account for the seam allowance.) This is the center line for plotting the border.

■ Cut and prepare appliqué pieces A, B and C as indicated on the templates.

■ Position the 24 units on the borders as shown.

■ Add 4 extra flowers on the ends of the side borders to fill in the corners.

■ Appliqué and add the borders to the quilt.

Quilting

This top wasn't quilted by our photography deadline. We plan to do some old-fashioned close quilting by hand (only time will tell if that gets done.)

Quilting the appliquéd border:

■ Note the quilting lines in the appliqué pattern. Many of the fancy 1930s appliqué quilts were quilted with lines about 3/8 of an inch inside the appliqué and an outline 3/8" away from the appliqué patch. Another option is quilting a line right in the ditch (covering the seam) of the appliqué.

■ Also note the quilted vine that fits between the appliqué and the outer border.

■ If you want the quilt to look as if it were quilted in the 1930s, you can fill the background in the border with a grid behind the appliqué. Use tape to mark a grid of 3/4" or 1" squares either parallel to the outside edge or on the diagonal.

On page 155 is a simple chain drawn with a 2 1/2" circle template that gives a period look to the sashing strips. And on page 156 is a quarter of a feathered wreath quilting pattern that fits into the corner triangles along the edge of the blocks. It can be traced, rotated and traced again to make a half sunflower that fits into the larger triangles along the edge. Quilting a grid of squares to fill the area behind the wreath will give the quilting an old-fashioned air.

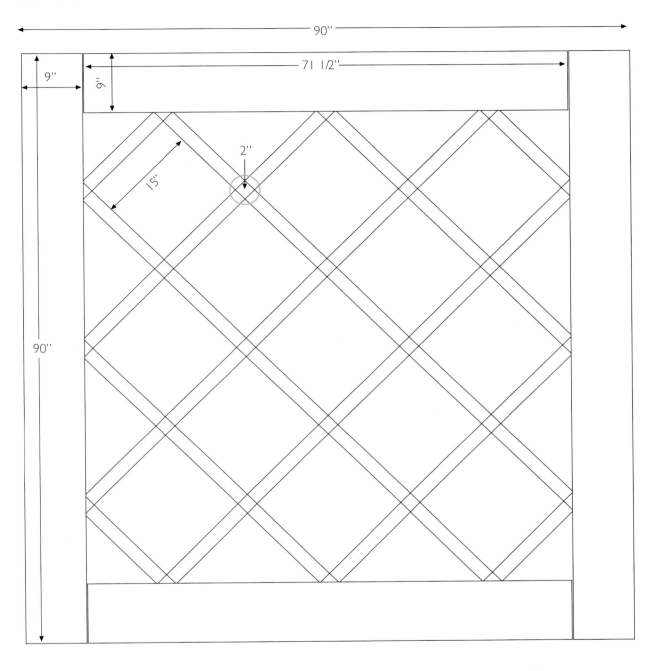

Illus. 14.12

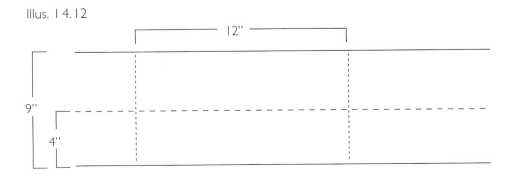

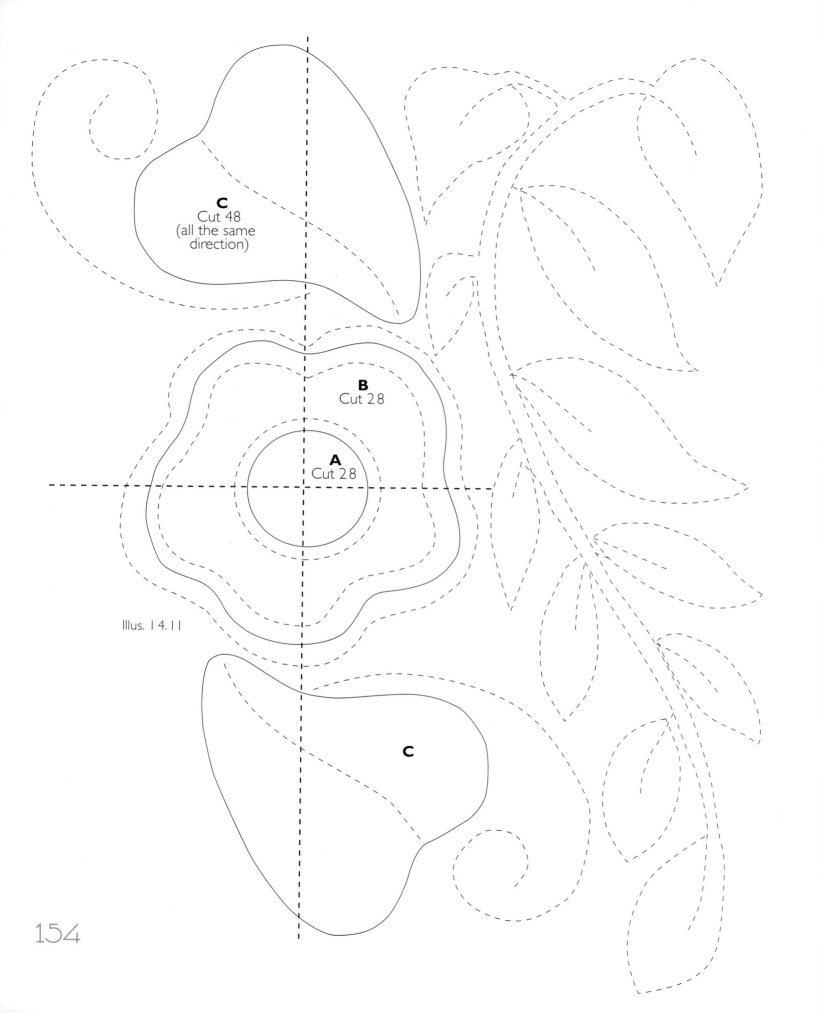

C
Cut 48
(all the same
direction)

B
Cut 28

A
Cut 28

Illus. 14.11

C

Illus. 14.13

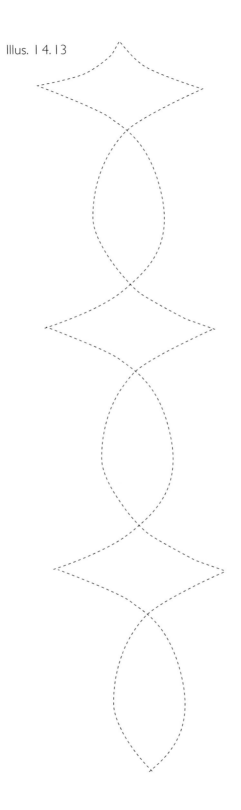

Illus. 14.14

156

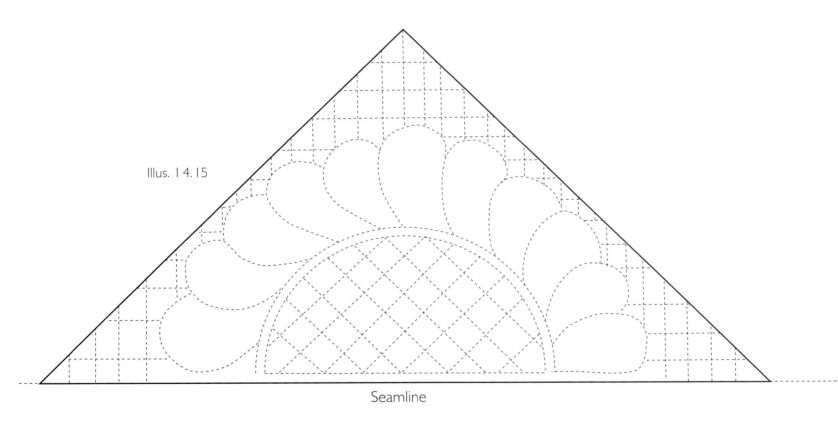

Illus. 14.15

Seamline

157

Fiesta Four Block. Hand appliquéd by Barbara Brackman, Lawrence, Kansas. 40" x 40". Machine quilted by Jeanne Zyck. The color scheme is derived from Barbara's collection of mid-century pottery, collectible dinnerware such as Metlox, Bauerware and Fiesta Ware, among others.

Fiesta Four Block

40" Quilt
15" Finished Blocks
4" Sashing
3" Border

Four of the basket blocks make a wall hanging or baby quilt. You can choose your favorite four or repeat a single basket as in this quilt made from the Cake Stand pattern in "Rose's Orchid." Barbara left out the appliquéd orchid, but added the floral appliqué in the center from "Kate's Wild Rose." Substitute your favorite florals for the center motif. Because the appliqué covers the seam lines, any of the flowers in the Designer Basket sampler will fit in the center.

You'll need:

- 4 Blocks Finishing to 15"
- 4" Sash
- 3" Border

Fabric Requirements

The Blocks:

- 4 fat Quarters (18 x 22") of yellow batik or bright prints, 4 of aqua or turquoise for the basket blocks. The prints are monochromatic, with figure and ground of the same color in different shades.
- 3 scraps of orange: 2 medium, 1 dark for the flowers.

The Border & Binding:

- 1 1/4 yards of yellow for the border (Barbara used a fifth yellow)
- 1/2 yard of one of the brightest yellows for the binding

Backing:

- 1 1/4 yards. 40" will probably fit into the width of a piece of fabric, so you won't need to piece it.

Cutting

The Blocks:

For cutting and sewing instructions for the Cake Stand blocks see page 106. Cut the large triangles "K" first from each fat quarter and use the rest for backgrounds and smaller triangles. Mix and match the yellows in each block for a scrappy look.

For the templates for the Wild Rose appliqué, which is added after the top is completed, see page 122. The flowers are two different medium oranges, the centers the same dark.

The Sashing

- Cut 2 strips 4 1/2" by 15 1/2" of yellow fabric.
- Cut 1 strip 4 1/2" by 34 1/2" of yellow.

The Border

- Cut 2 strips 3 1/2" by 40 1/2" of yellow for side borders.
- Cut 2 strips 3 1/2" by 34 1/2" of yellow for top & bottom borders.

Setting the Quilt

- Stitch the short sashing strips between the blocks as shown.
- Add the top and bottom borders and the long sashing strip.

- Add the side borders.
- Appliqué the floral design over the seams.

Quilting

Jeanne quilted half a feather wreath in the empty baskets, added more feathers in the backgrounds and gridded the basket with lines 1 1/2" apart. Reduce the feather wreath pattern on page 156 by about 50% for a pattern that would fit the empty baskets.

Illus. 14.21

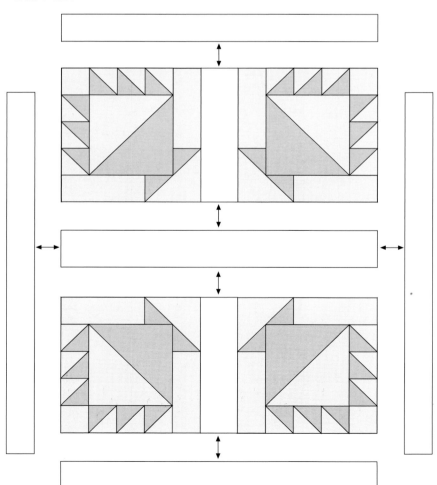

40"

34"

3"

4"

40"

15"

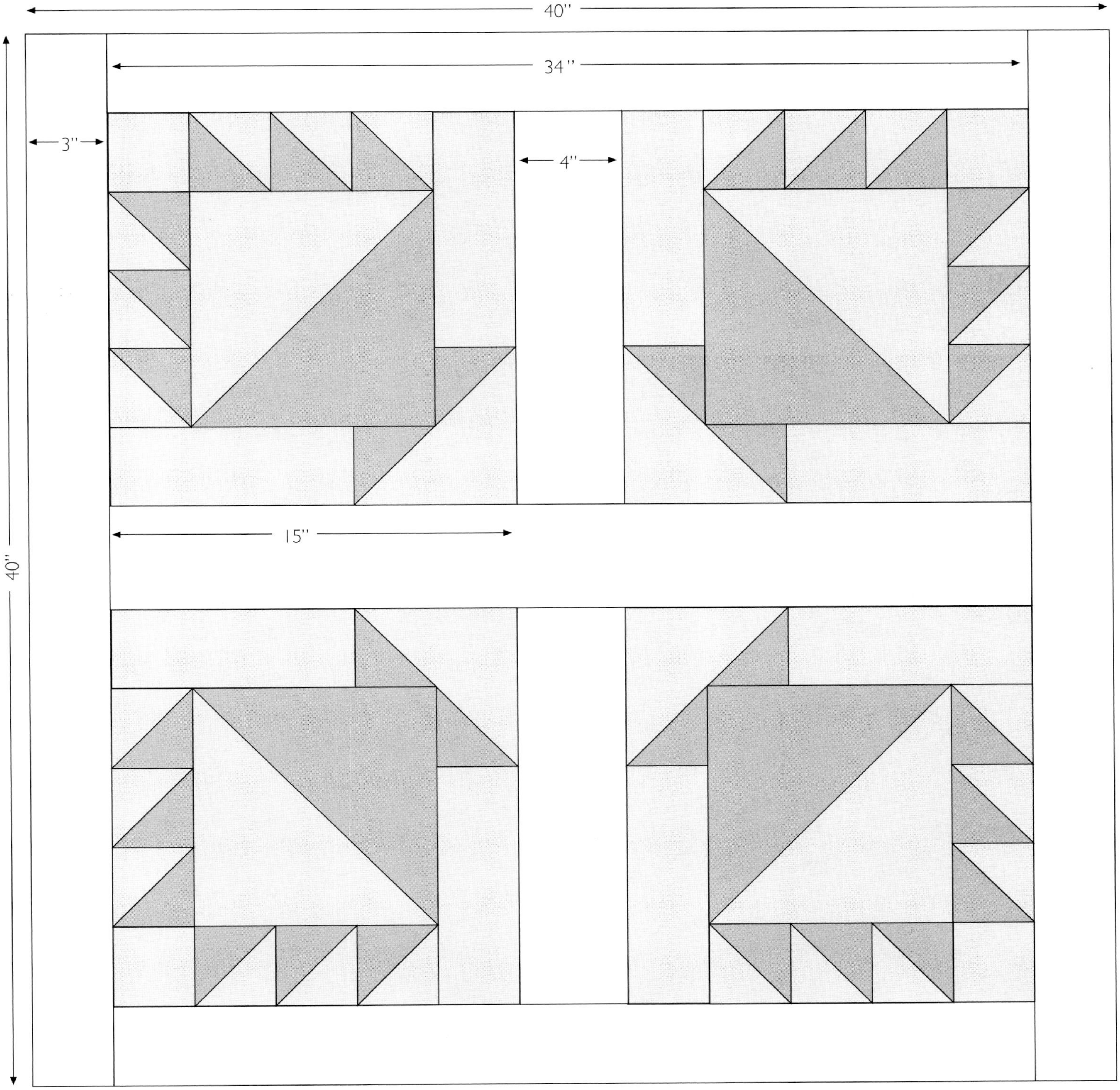

Raspberry-Lime Sorbet Spring Bouquets

Left, *Raspberry-Lime Sorbet Spring Bouquets,* hand appliquéd and hand quilted by Linda Kittle, Leavenworth Kansas. 50" x 50" Linda's vibrant color scheme calls to mind a summer meal served on a set of old Franciscan pottery. Her four-block quilt is pieced of "Kate's Wild Rose" blocks with a 4" sashing. She appliquéd 12 extra leaves in the sashing and bordered the blocks with 5 borders measuring 2", 1 1/2", a 1" check, 1 1/2" and 2".

Appliquéd Borders

Several of the model makers designed their own borders, making use of their favorite flowers from the blocks. Four corners show the diversity. Top is Shirley and Shirlene Wedd's, next Deb Lybarger's, third is the border designed by Barbara Brackman for the newspaper pattern and last is a double vine bordering a quilt called *The Autumn Years* by Linda Harker of Kansas City, Kansas.

Where the Wild Flowers Grow by Jean Pearson Stanclift, Lawrence, Kansas. Machine quilted by Lori Kukuk. 108" x 108". Jean machine appliquéd the date within a border of sawteeth and florals in her version of the series design. She based her palette on a tan ground, a decidedly 21st century color scheme.

Where the Wildflowers Grow

108" Quilt

15" Blocks

2" Sashing

9" Appliquéd border

3" Sawtooth border

6" Outer border

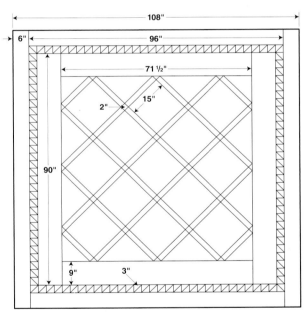

Setting the Quilt

Set the blocks with sashing in the same fashion as the Christmas baskets on page 138. Jean made the cornerstones the same fabric as the tan sashing strips. Her border is her own design, one that is not easily patterned for a book. Below we give you information that will help you design a similar border.

Fabric Requirements

Setting:

■ 2 yards of medium tan print for the sashing strips and cornerstones

■ 1 yard of light tan for the edge (or setting) triangles

Appliqué:

■ 4 quarter yard pieces (long or fat) of green prints for the various leaves

■ scraps from the blocks in purple, red, yellow and blue for the flowers

■ 1 yard of dark blue for the bias vine

Borders, Binding & Backing:

■ 2 1/2 yards of medium tan print for the appliqué border's background

■ 4 fat quarters of tan prints for the sawtooth border

■ 4 fat quarters of red prints for the sawtooth border

■ 3 1/4 yards of red print for the outer border and binding

■ 9 3/4 yards of backing to piece together a back

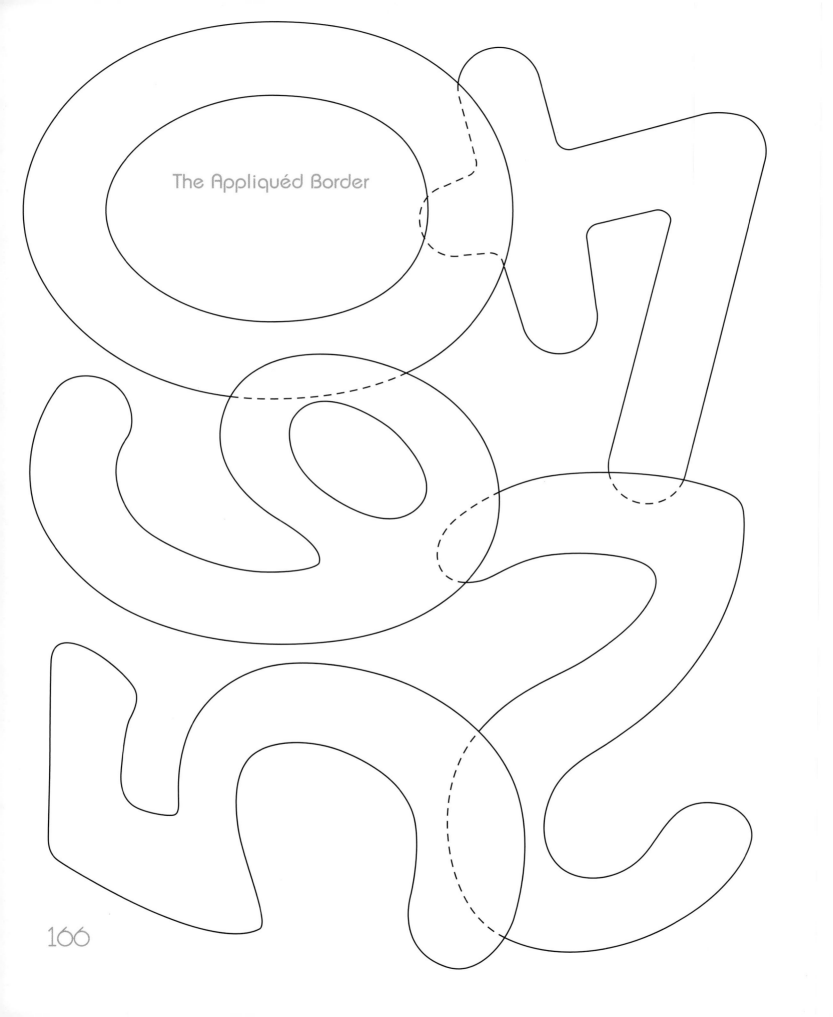

The Appliquéd Border

166

Cutting

The Background:

For the sides, cut 2 strips 9 1/2" by 90 1/2". For the top and bottom, cut 2 strips 9 1/2" by 72".
Note: It's important to measure your quilt before adding each border. Measure through the center of the quilt in both directions to make sure the borders and the quilt are the same length.

The Date:

We give you dates for the immediate future on page 166. Add a bit less than 1/4" for the seam allowance. One way to make a pattern for letters and numbers on your quilt is to type the figures in a word processing program using an interesting font and the largest type size you have. If you type the date 2005 in a 72 point type size, it will print out at 1" tall. Enlarge the figures by duplicating them on a photocopy machine at the maximum (200%) until they are about 5" tall.

The Flowers and Leaves:

Jean chose her favorites among the appliquéd flowers in the Designer Basket series. Cut the following pieces from the various baskets:
Chapter 1, McKim's flower and leaf: cut 3 of A, B and C; 6 of I
Chapter 7, Ver Mehren's tulip: Cut 1 of A and B.
Chapter 8, Sexton's leaf: Cut 16 of Q
Chapter 10, Hall's Iris, sunflower and leaf: Cut 2 of C and D; 3 of A and B and 6 of E (half one direction, half the other.)
Chapter 11, Capper's wild rose and leaf: Cut 4 A and B; 10 C.
Chapter 12, Farmer-Stockman's bluebells: Cut 6 E.
Chapter 13, Danner's leaf: Cut 51 E (either leaf.)

Jean also cut about a yard of green bias finishing to 3/8" for various stems to connect the flowers to the vine.

Bias Vine:

Cut from the dark blue about 11 yards of bias strip measuring 3/4" finished.

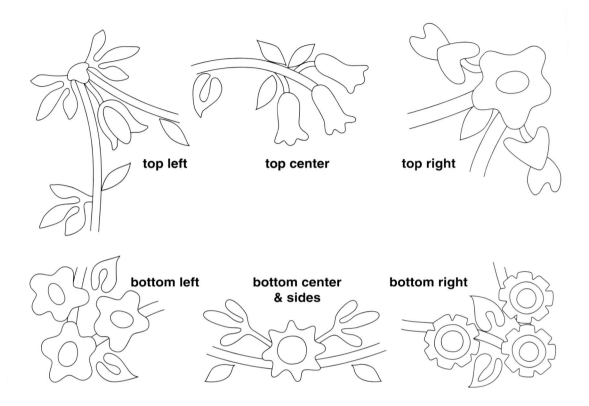

top left **top center** **top right**

bottom left **bottom center
& sides** **bottom right**

Positioning the Appliqué

Jean placed a sunflower in the center of each of the side borders and the bottom border. She placed the date in the top border. The floral group in each corner is different. See the diagrams for her corner arrangements. Begin by placing the corner designs and those in the center of each border. Pin or glue in place.

Position and secure the appliqué to the inner border before attaching it to the quilt.
Place a slightly curving vine of bias along the borders, growing out from the center designs and meeting under the corner designs. To place the bias strips, fold the edges under and press, pinning, gluing or basting the strips in place.

Jean added the various leaves in a symmetrical fashion to the left and right of the center. See the cover and the diagrams for suggestions on how to design your leaf arrangement.

After you have finished positioning and securing the pieces in place, appliqué using your favorite technique. Attach the top and bottom borders to the quilt top, then the sides, finishing the final appliqué that goes atop the seams after the borders are stitched in place.

The Sawtooth Border & the Outer Border

You'll need:

- 124 sawtooth squares finishing to 3"
- Red border strips 6" wide

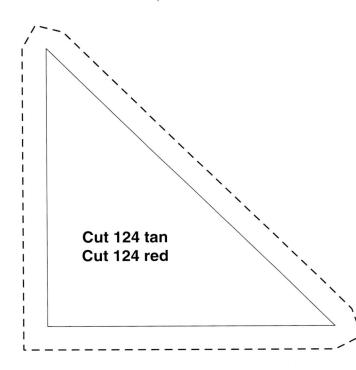

Cut 124 tan
Cut 124 red

Cutting:

- Use the template and cut the triangles as indicated, or rotary cut the triangles by cutting 62 squares 3 7/8" of varied reds and 62 of tan.
- Cut each square in half diagonally from corner to corner to make 2 triangles. You'll need 124 red and 124 tan triangles.
- Cut the outside border strips by cutting 2 strips 6 1/2" by 109" for the sides and 2 strips 6 1/2" by 97" for the top and bottom. Trim these strips if necessary when you are ready to add them.

Stitching

- Piece the triangles into sawtooth squares.
- Make 2 lengths of 30 sawtooth squares for the top and bottom borders.
- Make 2 lengths of 32 sawtooth squares for the side borders.
- Add the top and bottom sawtooth borders first; then the sides.
- Press.
- Add the top and bottom outer borders first, then the sides.
- Press.

Quilting

Lori machine-quilted a variety of designs, including a half of a feather wreath in the setting triangles and a chain similar to the one shown on page 155 in the sashing. Handquilters might want to use the quilting shown with the Designer Basket quilt on page 156.

Gallery

Red Hot Women of Design 64" x 64"
Kathy Delaney, Overland Park, Ks.
Machine quilted by Kelly Ashton

Designer Baskets 93" x 93" debi
schrader, Kansas City, Kansas
Machine quilted by Lee and Betty
Robertson

Kansas City Star Flower Basket 90 x 90"
Shirlene K. Wedd and Shirley C. Wedd,
Lawrence, Kansas

Midnight Flower Baskets 82"x 82"
Carol Kirchoff, Shawnee, Ks.
Machine quilted by Jeanne Zyck

Designer Baskets 90" x 90"
Pamela Mayfield, Lawrence, Ks.
Machine quilted by Lori Kukuk

Blessings in the Basket 80" x 80"
Susannah Christenson, Lawrence, Ks.

Gallery

Lotsa Dots 90" x 90"
Deb Rowden, Lawrence, Ks.

L to R: *Twilight Garden Baskets* by Amanda Gilbert, Manhattan, Ks., machine quilting by Linda Harker; four-block by Lisa Gray, Leavenworth, Ks.; and *Garden of Joy*, Denise Mariano, Leavenworth, Ks.

172

Bibliography

Below are the published sources for the biographies for the women (and the one man) of design.

To read more about Ruby McKim

Cuesta Benberry, "Missouri's Twentieth-Century Quilt Pattern Suppliers" *Ladies Circle Patchwork Quilts*, May, 1988

Jill Sutton-Filo, "Ruby Short McKim: The Formative Years" *Uncoverings 1996*, Volume 17. Editor, Virginia Gunn. (American Quilt Study Group, San Francisco, 1996)

Kim McKim, "Down Memory Lane," Reprint of *Designs Worth Doing # 1* (McKim Studios, Independence, 1979)

Louise O. Townsend, "*Kansas City Star* Patterns," *Uncoverings, 1984.* (Mill Valley, California: American Quilt Study Group, 1985)

To read more about Eveline Foland

Enola Gish, "News from the Quilt Lady," *Baldwin Ledger*, February, 28, 1985, pg. 6. (Wilene Smith's research)

Louise O. Townsend, "Eveline Foland: Quilt Pattern Illustrator," *Quilters Newsletter Magazine*, April, 1985, pp 20-23. "*Kansas City Star* Patterns," *Uncoverings, 1984. (Mill Valley, California:* American Quilt Study Group, 1985)

To read more about Edna Marie Dunn

Much of the information about Dunn and *The Kansas City Star* patterns is from research by Louise Townsend who interviewed Edna Marie Dunn Douglass in 1978 and corresponded with her niece, Shirley Mikesell. Louise Townsend, "The Meetin' Place: Edna Marie Dunn", *Quilters Newsletter Magazine, #107,* November/December, 1978. "*Kansas City Star* Patterns," *Uncoverings, 1984.* (Mill Valley, California: American Quilt Study Group, 1985.)

To read more about Aunt Martha and *Work Basket*

Barbara Brackman, Midwestern Pattern Sources *Uncoverings 1980*, Volume 1 (Mill Valley, California: American Quilt Study Group, 1981) 3-12.

To read more about Laura Wheeler

Wilene Smith, "Who Were Laura Wheeler & Alice Brooks?" *Quilters Newsletter Magazine, # 250*, March, 1993.

To read more about Hubert Ver Mehren

Susan Price Miller, "Hubert Ver Mehren and Home Art Studios," *Uncoverings 2000*, Volume 21 American Quilt Study Group, Lincoln, Nebraska, 2000. Pp. 107-136.

"The Medallion Man: Hubert Ver Mehren," *Century of Quilts, Better Homes and Gardens*, 2002. Pp. 60-61.

Edna Paris Ford, "Those Beautiful Home Art Studio Patterns," *Quilt World Omnibook*, #10, Spring, 1981.

Susan A. Murwin & Suzzy C. Payne, *The Quick and Easy Giant Dahlia Quilt* (New York: Dover Publications, 1983)

To read more about Carlie Sexton

Susan Price Miller, "Carlie Sexton and Her Quilt Pattern Business", *Uncoverings 1996*, Volume 17 (San Francisco: American Quilt Study Group, 1996) 29-62.

"Carlie Sexton," *Century of Quilts* (Des Moines: Meredith Corp., 2002) 42-3.

To read more about Rose Kretsinger

Barbara Brackman, "Emporia, 1925-1950: Reflections on a Community," *Kansas Quilts and Quilters* (Lawrence: University Press of Kansas, 1993)

To read more about Carrie Hall

Barbara Brackman, "Madam Carrie Hall," *Quilters' Newsletter Magazine*, June, 1981.

Carrie Hall and Rose Kretsinger, *Romance of the Patchwork Quilt in America* (Caldwell, Idaho: Caxton Printers, 1935)

Bettina Havig, *Carrie Hall Blocks* (Paducah, Kentucky: American Quilters Society, 1999)

To read more about Louise Fowler Roote

Barbara Brackman, "Midwestern Pattern Sources," *Uncoverings 1980*, Volume 1 (Mill Valley, California: American Quilt Study Group, 1981) 3-12.

Louise Fowler Roote, introduction to *Kate's Blue Ribbon Quilts*, Famous Features, 1971.

To read more about Scioto Danner

Helen Ericson, "Who Is Mrs. Danner?" *Ladies Circle Patchwork Quilts*, June, July, 1987.

Margaret I. Smith, "Quilting Hobby Brings Profit," *Kansas City Star*, July 24, 1955.

"A Quilt Hobby Pays," *The Kansas City Star*, October 29, 1934.

"Quilting is a Fine Art," *El Dorado Times*, April 19, 1958

Kansas City Star Quilt Books

- Star Quilts I : One Piece At A Time
- Star Quilts II : More Kansas City Star Quilts
- Star Quilts III : Outside the Box
- Star Quilts IV : Prairie Flower: A Year On The Plains
- Star Quilts V : The Sister Blocks
- Star Quilts VI : Kansas City Quiltmakers
- Star Quilts VII : O'Glory: Americana Quilt Blocks from The Kansas City Star
- Star Quilts VIII : Hearts & Flowers: Hand Appliqué From Start to Finish
- Star Quilts IX : Roads & Curves Ahead
- Star Quilts X : Celebration of American Life: Appliqué Patterns Honoring a Nation and Its People*
- Star Quilts XI : Women of Grace & Charm: A Quilting Tribute to the Women Who Served in World War II*
- Star Quilts XII : A Heartland Album: More Techniques in Hand Appliqué
- Star Quilts XIII : Quilting A Poem: Designs Inspired by America's Poets
- Star Quilts XIV : Carolyn's Paper-Pieced Garden: Patterns for Miniature and Full-Sized Quilts
- Star Quilts XV : Murders On Elderberry Road: Mystery Book
- Star Quilts XVI : Friendships in Bloom: Round Robin Quilts
- Star Quilts XVII : Baskets of Treasures: Designs Inspired by Life Along the River
- Star Quilts XVIII : Heart & Home: Unique American Women and the Houses that Inspire
- Star Quilts XIX : Women of Design
- Star Quilts XX : The Basics : An Easy Guide to Beginning Quiltmaking
- Star Quilts XXI : Four Block Quilts: Echoes of History, Pieced Boldly & Appliquéd Freely
- Star Quilts XXII: No Boundaries: Bringing Your Fabric Over the Edge
- Star Quilts XXIII: Horn of Plenty for a New Century

Project books:

- Santa's Parade of Nursery Rhymes
- Fan Quilt Memories: A Selection of Fan Quilts from The Kansas City Star

Notes

Notes

Notes